50 WALKS IN
Brecon Beacons
& South Wales

50 Walks in Brecon Beacons & South Wales

Published by AA Publishing (a trading name of AA Media Limited, whose registered office is Grove House, Lutyens Close, Lychpit, Basingstoke, Hampshire RG24 8AG; registered number 06112600)

© AA Media Limited 2024
Fourth edition
First published 2003

Mapping in this book is derived from the following products:
OS Landranger 145 (walks 1, 15, 16)
OS Landranger 147 (walks 23–25)
OS Landranger 157 (walks 2–11)
OS Landranger 158 (walks 12, 13)
OS Landranger 159 (14, 17–21)
OS Landranger 160 (walks 22, 32–39)
OS Landranger 161 (walks 26–31, 46–50)
OS Landranger 162 (walk 45)
OS Landranger 170 (walk 40, 41)
OS Landranger 171 (walks 42–44)
OS Explorer 12 (walk 22)
OS Explorer 13 (walk 31)
OS Explorer 36 (walk 9)

© Crown copyright and database rights 2024 Ordnance Survey. 100021153.

Maps contain data available from openstreetmap.org © under the Open Database License found at opendatacommons.org

ISBN: 978-0-7495-8370-5
ISBN: 978-0-7495-8380-4 (SS)

A CIP catalogue record for this book is available from the British Library.

AA Media would like to thank the following contributors in the preparation of this guide:
Clare Ashton, Tracey Freestone, Lauren Havelock, Nicky Hillenbrand, Lin Hutton, Graham Jones, Ian Little, Richard Marchi, Nigel Phillips and Victoria Samways.

Cover design by
berkshire design company

Printed and bound in the UK by Oriental Press, Dubai.

A05851

We would like to thank the following photographers, companies and picture libraries for their assistance in the preparation of this book. Abbreviations for the picture credits are as follows:
Alamy = Alamy Stock Photo
Trade Cover, Michael Roberts Photography/Alamy
Special Cover, Alistair Heap/Alamy; Back Cover Advert, SolStock/ istockphoto; 12/13, stocker123/Alamy; 29, Christopher Nicholson/Alamy; 43, shoults/Alamy; 75, Stephen Davies/ Alamy; 94/95, Robin Weaver/Alamy; 117, Vit Javorik/Alamy; 127, Roger Donovan/ Alamy; 149, Ion Mes/Alamy; 176, SolStock/istockphoto

The contents of this book are believed correct at the time of printing. Nevertheless, the publishers cannot be held responsible for any errors or omissions or for changes in the details given in this book or for the consequences of any reliance on the information it provides. This does not affect your statutory rights. We have tried to ensure accuracy in this book, but things do change and we would be grateful if readers would advise us of any inaccuracies they may encounter by emailing walks@aamediagroup.co.uk

We have done our best to make sure that these walks are safe and achievable by walkers with a basic level of fitness. However, we can accept no responsibility for any loss or injury incurred while following the walks. Advice on walking safely can be found on pages 10–11.

Some of the walks may appear in other AA books and publications.

Discover and book AA-rated places to stay at www.RatedTrips.com.

AA

50 WALKS IN
Brecon Beacons
& South Wales

CONTENTS

How to use this book   6

Exploring the area   8

Walking in safety   10

The walks

HOW TO USE THIS BOOK

Each walk starts with an information panel giving all the information you will need about the walk at a glance, including its relative difficulty, distance and total amount of ascent. Difficulty levels and gradients are as follows:

Difficulty of walk

● Easy

● Intermediate

● Hard

Gradient

▲ Some slopes

▲▲ Some steep slopes

▲▲▲ Several very steep slopes

Maps

Every walk has its own route map. We also suggest a relevant Ordnance Survey map to take with you, allowing you to view the area in more detail. The time suggested is the minimum for reasonably fit walkers and doesn't allow for stops.

Route map legend

---▶---	Walk route		▦	Built-up area
❶	Route waypoint		▦	Woodland area
– – – –	Adjoining path		🚾	Toilet
•	Place of interest		P	Car park
⌂	Steep section		⊞	Picnic area
☀	Viewpoint		)(	Bridge
⸗⸗⸗⸗⸗	Embankment			

Start points

The start of each walk is given as a six-figure grid reference prefixed by two letters referring to a 100km square of the National Grid. More information on grid references can be found on most OS Walker's Maps.

Dogs

We have tried to give dog owners useful advice about how dog friendly each walk is. Please respect other countryside users. Keep your dog under control, especially around livestock, and obey local by-laws and other dog control notices.

Car parking

Many of the car parks suggested are public, but occasionally you may have to park on the roadside or in a lay-by. Please be considerate about where you leave your car, ensuring that you are not on private property or access roads, and that gates are not blocked and other vehicles can pass safely.

Walks locator map

EXPLORING THE AREA

There is no specific line on a map and there is no archetypal landscape or terrain that defines South Wales. More than anything, South Wales defines itself by its variety and its contrasts. From beach to mountain, cathedral to chapel, villain to saint and common to capital, the only parity is the disparity. The common thread is that they all have their beauties and they will all capture your imagination.

A Tale of Two Parks

The majority of the walks in this book are centred on the area's two National Parks. The Pembrokeshire Coast alone boasts over 180 miles (290km) of coastal path, but this doesn't tell the whole story. The history, adorned with myths and legends of the saints and kings of Wales fills in some of the gaps, though it still says little about the wildlife. Seabirds, seals and porpoises vie for your attention, while falcons share the flower-carpeted cliff tops with a host of other fascinating creatures.

Bannau Brycheiniog (Brecon Beacons)

The Park reclaimed its Welsh name of Bannau Brycheiniog (pronounced Ban-eye Bruck-ein-iog), or informally, the Bannau, on the 66th anniversary of the Park's designation. Its central peaks boast the highest ground in southern Britain and their tabletop summits preside over some of the finest upland scenery this country can offer. To the east, the Black Mountains are a hill-walkers paradise; their lumbering whaleback ridges and deeply cloven valleys are riddled with tracks and trails that make exploration both safe and easy. The two westernmost ranges, Fforest Fawr and the Black Mountain (singular), are a very different proposition, composed mainly of huge tracts of moorland which, on the whole, fall slightly outside the domain of this book. We have however, suggested some of the easier options available, including a tour of the incomparable Waterfall Country and a circuit around the formidable crags of the Carmarthen Fan.

The majority of the land is privately owned, but around 14 per cent belongs to the National Park Authority, 8 per cent to the Forestry Commission and around 4 per cent is in the hands of the National Trust. The National Park Authority, which is made up of a committee of both locally and nationally appointed members, is administered in Brecon, with a staff of over 100 people. The principle aim of the park, in common with all British National Parks, is to balance the needs of the landscape and the environment with the demands of visitors and the well-being of local communities.

The Best of South Wales

The remainder of the walks showcase other favourite areas of South Wales, and cherry-pick the best of the Gower coast, visiting swathes of golden sand embedded in jagged limestone cliffs, and sample a beautiful stretch of the Glamorgan Heritage Coast.

No book on this region would be complete without a mention of the Valleys and, of course, the industries that formed their tightly knit communities. Few landscapes have altered more radically in recent decades and the revitalised hilltops now make for some good walking. This book also touches on the capital, Cardiff, making an invigorating tour from a fairy-tale castle, just a few miles from the centre. Finally, the region's boundaries have been stretched as far as possible. To the north, it includes the austere charms of Abergwesyn Common, a definite walk on the wild side and once the last stand of the beautiful red kite. And east, to the border, to follow the lazy line of the meandering River Wye through some stunning deciduous woodland. Enjoy discovering the history, beauty and wildlife of this fascinating area.

PUBLIC TRANSPORT

Most of the walks in the book return to their original starting point. Unfortunately, these starting points are often in rural areas where there is little or no public transport. Any bus routes will likely have different timetables at weekends, bank holidays and in the winter. For public transport information, visit at www.traveline.cymru.

WALKING IN SAFETY

All these walks are suitable for any reasonably fit person, but less experienced walkers should try the easier walks first. Route-finding is usually straightforward, but you will find that an Ordnance Survey walking map is a useful addition to the route maps and descriptions; recommendations can be found in the information panels.

Risks

Although each walk here has been researched with a view to minimising the risks to the walkers who follow its route, no walk in the countryside can be considered to be completely free from risk. Walking in the outdoors will always require a degree of common sense and judgement to ensure that it is as safe as possible.

- Be particularly careful on cliff paths and in upland terrain, where the consequences of a slip can be very serious.

- Remember to check tidal conditions before walking on the seashore.

- Some sections of route are by, or cross, busy roads. Take care, and remember that traffic is a danger even on minor country lanes.

- Be careful around farmyard machinery and livestock, especially if you have children with you.

- Be aware of the consequences of changes in the weather, and check the forecast before you set out. Carry spare clothing and a torch if you are walking in the winter months. Remember that the weather can change very quickly at any time of the year, and in moorland and heathland areas, mist and fog can make route-finding much harder. Don't set out in these conditions unless you are confident of your navigation skills in poor visibility.

- In summer remember to take account of the heat and sun; wear a hat and carry water.

- On walks away from centres of population you should carry a whistle and survival bag. If you do have an accident that means you require help from the emergency services, make a note of your position as accurately as possible and dial 999.

Countryside Code
Respect other people:

- Consider the local community and other people enjoying the outdoors.

- Co-operate with people at work in the countryside. For example, keep out of the way when farm animals are being gathered or moved, and follow directions from the farmer.

- Don't block gateways, driveways or other paths with your vehicle.
- Leave gates and property as you find them, and follow paths unless wider access is available, such as on open country or registered common land (known as 'open access land').
- Leave machinery and farm animals alone – don't interfere with animals, even if you think they're in distress. Try to alert the farmer instead.
- Use gates, stiles or gaps in field boundaries if you can – climbing over walls, hedges and fences can damage them and increase the risk of farm animals escaping.
- Our heritage matters to all of us – be careful not to disturb ruins and historic sites.

Protect the natural environment:
- Take your litter home. Litter and leftover food don't just spoil the beauty of the countryside; they can be dangerous to wildlife and farm animals. Dropping litter and dumping rubbish are criminal offences.
- Leave no trace of your visit, and take special care not to damage, destroy or remove features such as rocks, plants and trees.
- Keep dogs under effective control, making sure they are not a danger or nuisance to farm animals, horses, wildlife or other people.
- If cattle or horses chase you and your dog, it is safer to let your dog off the lead – don't risk getting hurt by trying to protect it. Your dog will be much safer if you let it run away from a farm animal in these circumstances, and so will you.
- Everyone knows how unpleasant dog mess is and it can cause infections, so always clean up after your dog and get rid of the mess responsibly – bag it and bin it.
- Fires can be as devastating to wildlife and habitats as they are to people and property – so be careful with naked flames and cigarettes at any time of the year.

Enjoy the outdoors:
- Plan ahead and be prepared for natural hazards, changes in weather and other events.
- Wild animals, farm animals and horses can behave unpredictably if you get too close, especially if they're with their young – so give them plenty of space.
- Follow advice and local signs.

For more information visit www.gov.uk/government/publications/the-countryside-code

A WALK ABOVE NEWPORT

DISTANCE/TIME	5.5 miles (8.8km) / 3hrs 30min
ASCENT/GRADIENT	1,080ft (329m) / ▲ ▲ ▲
PATHS	Easy coastal footpaths, boggy farm tracks, rough paths over bracken and heather-covered hillsides
LANDSCAPE	Attractive harbour, farmland and rock-capped moor
SUGGESTED MAP	OS Explorer OL35 North Pembrokeshire
START/FINISH	Grid reference: SN057392
DOG FRIENDLINESS	Care on roads, poop scoop on coast path section
PARKING	Car park opposite information centre in Long Street
PUBLIC TOILETS	At start and also in Parrog car park

Carn Ingli appears to peep over the shoulder of the small coastal town of Newport in the same way as Table Mountain does in Cape Town, South Africa. The domination of the town's skyline by the bold, rock-capped summit seems to make them inseparable and it therefore makes sense to explore both in one walk. The coastal section is easy to follow and thoroughly enjoyable as the path traces a varied line along the Nyfer Estuary, at one stage following the actual sea wall itself. The tracks that cross the common, on the other hand, are rough and, in late summer, when the bracken is fully grown, difficult to follow in places. They're worth sticking with though, for the views from the jagged rocks of the peak are among the best in the whole of the Pembrokeshire Coast National Park.

Once a busy port immersed predominantly in the wool trade, Newport was the former capital of the Marcher Lordship of Cemmaes, the only one to escape the abolition imposed by Henry VIII in the 16th-century Acts of Union. William Fitz-Martin, who moved to Newport from nearby Nevern, granted a number of privileges to the town, including the election of its own mayor, something which it still has to this day, and the beating of the bounds on horseback by the mayor, which takes place every August. Its castle, once the home of the aforementioned lord, has since been incorporated into a mansion house and is now in private ownership.

Often described as one of the most sacred sites in Britain, the lofty heights of Carn Ingli were well known by the mystical St Brynach, who scaled them in order to commune with angels. After a life of persecution – the Irish-born saint was made most unwelcome by the Welsh when he returned from his pilgrimage to the Holy Land – he finally settled in Nevern, where he built his church. It remains one of the most visited in Pembrokeshire due to its ancient Celtic cross and a yew tree that appears to actually bleed. A second cross, carved into the rocky hillside, has seen so many visitors that the stones beneath it are now as smooth as glass. Judging from the remains of both Iron Age fortresses and Bronze Age huts, there was human activity on Mynydd Carningli long before Christianity. The size of the settlements suggests that the windswept hillside would have once supported fairly large communities. Perhaps the existence of standing stones near by demonstrates that these early settlers were also aware of the mountain's special powers.

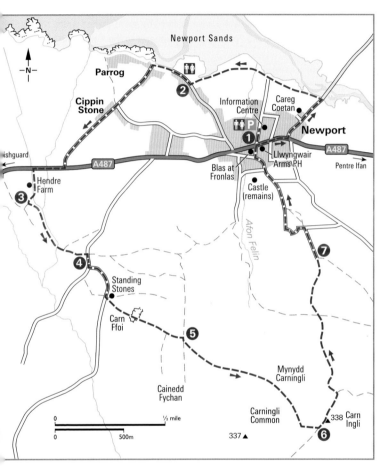

1. Turn right out of the car park in Long Street and left on to East Street (A487). Fork left into Pen y Bont and continue to the bridge, where a way-marked footpath leads off to the left. Follow this along the banks of the estuary to a small road.

2. Turn right on the road and walk past the toilets to its end, where the path then follows the sea wall. Continue to another lane and turn left to follow it up to the A487. Turn right on to this road, then turn left to continue walking up the drive of Hendre farm.

3. Pass the farmhouse on your right to go through the gate and follow the track to another gate where you turn left to follow a small stream. The path emerges on to open ground and hugs the left edge of the field to reach

another gate. Continue in the same line along a hedged section, which is boggy for most of the year. Climb over a stile and keep straight ahead to climb up to the road.

4. Turn right on to the road and then fork left to continue past some houses to a pair of huge upright stones on the left. Pass through these stones and follow the faint track up to a rocky tor. Head up from this towards the larger tor of Carn Ffoi. From the top of here you'll be able to pick up a clearer path that leads through an old field system defined by small, ruined walls. Navigate your way through the old fields heading southeast to the right-hand side of a fenced field.

5. Now bear half right onto a clear footpath (to the left of the path that runs between lines of low gorse) that leads across the hillside, aiming towards the obvious top of Carn Ingli, which will come into view as you climb. Fork left after 50yds (46m) and then continue across the hillside beneath the high point of Carningli Common. The path bears right to climb into the saddle between Carningli Common and the rocky top of Mynydd Carningli. Continue to the far end of the rocky ridge and then bear left to follow a faint path up on to the ridge top.

6. Carry on to Carn Ingli and bear left along the path to pass in front of it, to join a good, clear track that runs straight down the hillside. Continue on this, keeping straight ahead at two crossroads. This drops you down to a gate in a corner, where a path leads on to a concrete track.

7. Take the lane to a T-junction and turn left. Follow this road down to a junction in College Square, where you turn left. This is Church Street. Continue into the centre and turn right into Market Street to the main road, which you cross into Long Street.

Where to eat and drink
The Llwyngwair Arms is one of the best pubs in the area, with good beer and a local but friendly atmosphere. Blas at Fronlas in Market Street is a great place for a snack or a cuppa.

What to see
On your left, as you approach the bridge along Pen-y-Bont, you'll find the rather understated Careg Coetan, an impressive cromlech or burial chamber tucked away behind holiday bungalows. As with many such sites in Wales, it's said to be the final resting place of King Arthur.

While you're there
Small lanes lead east from Newport to Pentre Ifan, one of the finest megalithic cromlechs in the British Isles. Over 4,000 years old, the giant 16ft (4.8m) capstone sits on a selection of smaller supports that hold it some 6ft (1.8m) above ground. It is thought that the builders of these magnificent tombs believed by constructing them on high ground the interred souls of the dead would be placed closer to the spirits and the bringer of life, the sun. It would have originally been covered with a mound of earth, but this has since eroded away.

AROUND DINAS HEAD

DISTANCE/TIME	3 miles (4.8km) / 2hrs
ASCENT/GRADIENT	460ft (140m) / ▲ ▲ ▲
PATHS	Rough coastal path and a short section of easy, wheelchair-friendly track
LANDSCAPE	Rugged cliffs with views over two sweeping bays
SUGGESTED MAP	OS Explorer OL35 North Pembrokeshire
START/FINISH	Grid reference: SN004399
DOG FRIENDLINESS	Care on cliff tops and around livestock
PARKING	By The Old Sailors, Pwllgwaelod Beach
PUBLIC TOILETS	In car park at the start and in car park at Cwm-yr-Eglwys

Dinas Island, or Dinas Head as it's often known (Dinas Head is actually the headland at the island's northern apex), isn't actually an island at all. It's a rugged, sloping peninsula that's separated from the mainland by a shallow neck of flat marshy ground known as Cwm Dewi ('David's valley'). This was formed at the end of the last ice age when a glacier blocked the outlet of Newport Bay, forcing watercourses westwards, beneath the ice. The shales and sandstones of the headland were eroded into a narrow channel. Island or not, this is a wonderful place to walk, encapsulating everything that's great about walking along a coast path for an hour or so's effort. In springtime, there's the added bonus of carpets of luscious bluebells in the woods.

The ruins of the tiny chapel of St Brynach dominate a pleasant green above the beach. Sheltered from the prevailing southwesterly winds that pound this stretch of coast, Cwm-yr-Eglwys ('valley of the church') often has the feel of a quaint Mediterranean hamlet, but on the night of 25 October 1859 it was subjected to one of the fiercest storms on record and the church was very badly knocked about. However, this was only a small part of the damage wreaked. That same fearful night, 114 ships were wrecked off the Welsh coast, with the loss of many lives. Another storm in 1979 all but completed the job of destruction – all that is left of the church today are the west wall and the tiny belfry. The saint to whom the chapel was dedicated probably came from Ireland where he would have been known as Bernach. According to the account of his life, written in the 12th century, he lived in the 6th century and visited both Rome and Brittany before arriving at what is now Milford Haven. He set about establishing various oratories in the area as well as a monastery at Nanhyfer, where he was to die. Along the way, he had many adventures, including being wounded by a spear but escaping with his life due to the timely intervention of his travelling companions. It's said he went on to have a visitation from an angel and performed various miracles, thus ensuring his posthumous rise to sainthood.

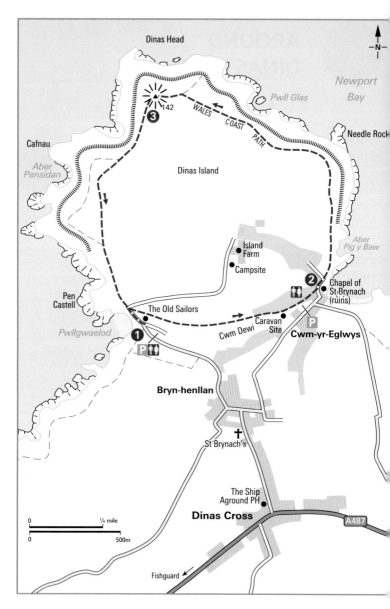

1. From the car park, make your way to the beach and bear right and then immediately right again, through a gate, to gain a well-surfaced path that follows the floor of Cwm Dewi. This wheelchair-friendly track is very popular so you'll probably meet other walkers as you pass the marshy ground to the right. These marshes are important breeding grounds for several butterflies, such as tortoiseshells, peacocks, common blues and orange-tips. The path leads to a gate that in turn leads you through a caravan site and into the Cwm-yr-Eglwys car park. Turn left in the car park and follow a narrow path, which heads out towards the beach.

2. Keep the ruins to your right and wander along the lane to a coast path waymarker on the right. Follow this steeply up steps to Aber Pig-y-Baw. The path emerges from the bushes and continues to cut easily around the hillside before steepening as it approaches the obvious sea stack of Needle Rock. Ignore the footpath off to the left before this. This is a fine nesting site for a variety of seabirds and it appears positively congested in late spring and early summer. Steps lead up the hillside to a gate from here and then the path continues to climb for over half a mile (800m) to the trig point that marks the top of the headland. This is a wonderfully lofty viewpoint and it is possible to scramble down a little way to the north if you fancy a sheltered rest stop.

3. The path now leads down above the western cliffs. Stay on the outside of the perimeter fence as it swings south again. Follow the coast down and wind your way through the gorse to a fork where you bear right (ignoring the yellow arrow pointing to the left) to the spur of Pen Castell. This tracks back inland again and drops to a gate above Pwllgwaelod Beach. From here you reach the road and can walk easily back past the Old Sailors restaurant to the beach and the car park.

Where to eat and drink

The Old Sailors licensed restaurant, adjacent to the car park, has replaced a pub called the Sailor's Safety Inn, which once showed a light to guide shipping. It specialises in seafood but it's also a good spot for a cream tea if that's all you need. Away from here, there's the popular Ship Aground, a grand public house in nearby Dinas Cross.

What to see

The black and white birds usually seen on the steeper inner cliff of Needle Rock are guillemots and razorbills. Both are members of the auk family and it is difficult to tell them apart from a distance. The guillemot is actually a beautiful dark-chocolate colour and has a slim pointed bill, while the razorbill is more black in colour and close inspection of the head reveals that the bill is razor shaped, with thin white lines. You'll probably also notice a number of herring gulls on the fringes of the mêlée. These raucous gulls scavenge relentlessly, feeding on the eggs and chicks of the smaller auks. They will even steal the food from the parent birds' mouths.

While you're there

Check out the Saints and Stones Trail, a waymarked driving tour of some of the finest churches and religious sites in the area, many dating back to pre-Christian times. As well as St Davids Cathedral, other highlights include the bleeding yew in St Brynach's. Leaflets describing the trail, which makes a big loop between Fishguard and St Davids, are available from all the local tourist offices.

AROUND STRUMBLE HEAD

DISTANCE/TIME	8 miles (12.9km) / 3hrs 30min
ASCENT/GRADIENT	920ft (280m) / ▲ ▲ ▲
PATHS	Coastal path, grassy, sometimes muddy tracks, rocky paths, many stiles
LANDSCAPE	Rugged headland, secluded caves and rocky tor
SUGGESTED MAP	OS Explorer OL35 North Pembrokeshire
START/FINISH	Grid reference: SM894411
DOG FRIENDLINESS	Care needed near cliff tops and livestock
PARKING	Car parks by Strumble Head Lighthouse
PUBLIC TOILETS	None on route

This is a wonderful stretch of the Pembrokeshire coast, although at times it feels like 'coast path meets the Himalayas', as the narrow ribbon of trail climbs and drops at regular intervals throughout. This is the real wild side of Pembrokeshire.

The headland cliffs tower above the pounding Atlantic surf, the path cuts an airy, at times precarious, line across their tops and the sky is alive with the sound of seabirds. Atlantic grey seals, porpoises and even dolphins are regularly spotted in the turbulent waters. Garn Fawr, a formidable rocky tor that lords it high above the whole peninsula, brings a touch of hill walking to the experience, and the shapely lighthouse flashes a constant reminder of just how treacherous these spectacular waters can be.

Built in 1908 to help protect the ferries that run between Fishguard and Ireland, the Strumble Head Lighthouse guards a hazardous stretch of coast that wrecked at least 60 ships in the 19th century alone. The revolving lights, which flash four times every 15 seconds, were originally controlled by a massive clockwork system that needed rewinding every 12 hours. This was replaced in 1965 by an electrically powered system and the lighthouse was then converted to unstaffed operation in 1980. It's possible to cross the daunting narrow chasm that separates Ynys Meicel (St Michael's Island), where the lighthouse stands, from the mainland by a rickety bridge.

This is one of the best walks in Pembrokeshire to spot Atlanic grey seals – they can reach over 8ft (2.4m) in length and can weigh as much as 770lbs (350kg). They are usually seen bobbing up and down (bottling) in the water just off the coast, but in autumn when the females give birth to a single pup, they often haul up on to inaccessible beaches where the young are suckled on milk with an incredibly high fat content. The pups shed their white coats after around three weeks, when they are then weaned and taught to swim. The males are usually bigger than the females, with a darker coat and a much more pronounced nose. The best places to see seals on this walk are the bays of Pwll Bach and Pwlluog, near the start.

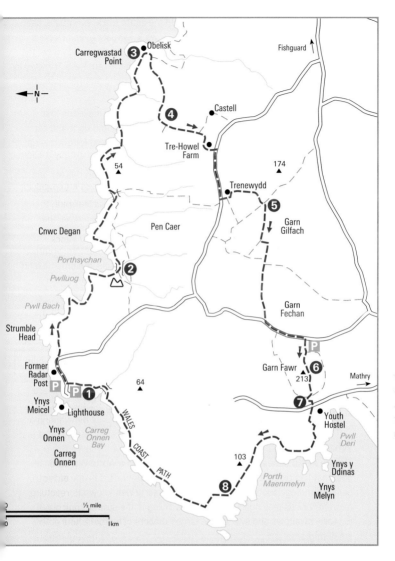

1. Walk back up the road from the car park and cross a gate on the left on to the coast path. Pass above the bays of Pwll Bach and Pwlluog, then drop steeply to a footbridge behind the pebble beach of Porthsychan.

2. Follow the coast path waymarkers around Cnwc Degan and down to another bridge, where a couple of footpaths lead away from the coast. Continue along the coast, passing a cottage on the right and climbing and dropping several times, before you reach the obelisk at Carregwastad Point.

3. Follow the main path inland and turn right then bear left. Continue with this path, which is vague in places, up through the gorse to a wall, then turn right to walk the length of a field to a stile and go on to a good track. Take this through a succession of gates and around a left-hand bend.

4. Ignore a track to the right and continue up the cattle track, eventually bearing right into the farmyard where you follow a walkway past livestock pens before swinging left, after the buildings, to the road. Turn right and follow the road past a large house to a waymarked bridleway on the left. Pass Trenewydd and go through a gate on to a green lane. Follow this up to another gate and on to open ground.

5. Turn right here and follow the wall to yet another gate. This leads to a walled track which you follow to the road. Turn left and climb up to the car park beneath Garn Fawr. Turn right, on to a hedged track, and follow this up, through a gap in the wall, and over rocks to the trig point.

6. Climb down and follow the path to cross the saddle between this tor and the other, slightly lower, one to the south. From here, head west towards an even lower out-crop and pass it on the left. Continue on this clear path that leads down to a stile. Cross this and turn left, then right on to a drive that leads to the road.

7. Walk straight across and on to the coast path. Bear right past the youth hostel and cross a stile to drop down towards Ynys y Ddinas, the small island ahead. Navigation is easy as you follow the coast path north, over Porth Maenmelyn and up to a cairn.

8. Continue along the coast, towards the lighthouse, until you return to the car park.

Where to eat and drink

The one down side about walking in such a wild spot is the lack of facilities. There is occasionally an ice cream van in the car park at the start. Failing that, there's the Farmers Arms in Mathry, further south, or head east towards Fishguard, where there's plenty of choice.

What to see

The small hut beneath the car park at the start was a World War II radar post that has been converted into a bird observatory. This is one of the best ornithology spots in the country, particularly well known for spotting migratory birds leaving in autumn and arriving in the spring. Look out for early swallows and swifts, also large numbers of warblers and other small migrants.

While you're there

At Carregwastad Point is a stone obelisk that marks the spot of the last hostile invasion of Britain. On 22 February 1797, a small French force known as the Legion Noire came ashore and set up camp at Tre-Howel, a local farm. The invaders were quick to take advantage of a huge haul of liquor that had been salvaged from a recent wreck and, subsequently unfit to fight, were forced to surrender within two days.

AROUND ST DAVIDS HEAD

DISTANCE/TIME	3.5 miles (5.7km) / 2hrs
ASCENT/GRADIENT	425ft (130m) / ▲
PATHS	Coast path, clear paths across heathland
LANDSCAPE	Dramatic cliffs, heather- and gorse-covered hillsides
SUGGESTED MAP	OS Explorer OL35 North Pembrokeshire
START/FINISH	Grid reference: SM734271
DOG FRIENDLINESS	Care needed on cliff tops and near livestock
PARKING	Whitesands Beach
PUBLIC TOILETS	At start of walk

It would be difficult to imagine a more atmospheric place than St Davids Head. For full effect, visit at sunset and watch the sky turn red over the scattered islets of the Bishops and Clerks.

Carn Llidi, a towering monolith of ancient rock that has all the attributes of a full-blown mountain, yet stands only 594ft (181m) above sea level, dominates the headland. Its heather- and gorse-covered flanks are alive with small heathland birds, which chatter from the swaying ferns and dart for cover in the hidden crannies of dry-stone walls. The coast, when you meet it, is at its intricate finest; a succession of deep and narrow inlets (known as zawns), broken up by stubborn headlands that thrust defiantly into the ever-present swells. The Head itself is magnificent and a few minutes spent exploring will quickly uncover a series of rocky terraces that offer shelter from the wind and stunning views over the ocean to Ramsey Island.

Despite its hostile demeanour, St Davids Head was once home to a thriving Iron Age community who lived in huts and kept their stock in a field system, the remains of which are still visible. The headland, naturally guarded by the ocean on three sides, was also defended by the Clawydd-y-Milwry (the Warrior's Dyke) at its eastern edge. The dyke is actually formed by three ditches and two ramparts that cut across the neck of the headland. The main bastion, a dry-stone wall that would have once stood around 15ft (4.6m) tall, is still easily visible as a linear pile of stones and rocks. Within the fort there are a number of standing stones, stone circles and the remains of basic huts. The defences are thought to have been built around AD 100.

At least 3,000 years older, and well worth seeking out, is Coetan Arthur, a neolithic quoit, or burial chamber, which stands directly above a narrow inlet, bounded on its eastern walls by the red-coloured crags of Craig Coetan, a popular climbing venue. Coetan Arthur consists of a 12ft (3.7m) capstone, propped up on a smaller rock. The quoit would have originally been covered with earth to form a mound, but this has long since been eroded away. There is evidence of several more burial chambers near the summit of Carn Llidi.

Both the headland and Carn Llidi are in the care of the National Trust, and you are free to wander at will to investigate these fascinating sites, although you should bear in mind that they are Scheduled Ancient Monuments and protected by law.

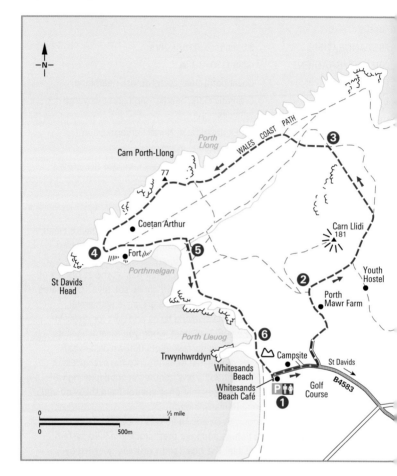

1. From Whitesands Beach head back up the road, pass the caravan site and immediately turn left along a road. Bear right where it splits and continue around a left-hand bend to walk up to the buildings. Keep left to walk between the buildings, then carry on to a gate.

2. Turn right shortly afterwards on to the open heathland and follow the footpath along the wall beneath Carn Llidi. Pass the track that drops to the youth hostel on the right and continue, keeping right wherever the track forks. Go over a crest and downhill to a corner of a wall where a clear track runs diagonally left towards the coast.

3. Follow this to the coast path, where there's a small fingerpost, and turn left to walk along the cliff tops. At Porth Llong, the path bears right to climb to a cairn. The headland is a labyrinth of paths and tracks, but for maximum enjoyment try to stick as close to the cliff tops as possible as you round a

number of narrow zawns. The official coast path doesn't go as far as the tip of the peninsula, but plenty of other tracks do, so follow one as far as you wish.

4. From the tip, turn left and make your way through the rocky outcrops on the southern side of the headland. As you approach Porthmelgan, you'll pick up an obvious path near the cliff tops which you should work your way down to using one of the many small paths.

5. This leads to a small footbridge over a stream, which you cross to climb up the steps on the other side. Continue to a kissing gate where the National Trust land ends and maintain your direction. Pass above Porth Lleuog and the distinctive rocky promontory of Trwynhwrddyn, which is worth a visit in its own right.

6. The path then drops steeply down to the road at the entrance to Whitesands Beach.

Where to eat and drink
Apart from a café serving light meals, snacks and drinks in the car park, the best place to eat and drink near this walk is St Davids itself. The Farmers Arms is the pick of the bunch, boasting a wonderful patio area, which can be a real suntrap on a summer afternoon. For coffee, try Pebbles Yard Gallery and Expresso Bar, in the centre.

What to see
The small islets west of the headland are the Bishops and Clerks. The northernmost and largest is North Bishop and the southernmost, crowned with a lighthouse, is South Bishop. The others all have individual names but are most often just referred to as the Clerks.

While you're there
The views from the rocky crest of Carn Llidi are among the finest on the whole coast – especially delightful at sunset. The easiest ascent is from the western side, where a broad track leads up the ridge past the ruined wartime buildings.

THE SHORES OF RAMSEY SOUND

DISTANCE/TIME	6 miles (9.7km) / 3hrs
ASCENT/GRADIENT	755ft (230m) / ▲ ▲
PATHS	Coast path and easy farmland tracks
LANDSCAPE	Undulating coast, dramatic views to Ramsey Island
SUGGESTED MAP	OS Explorer OL35 North Pembrokeshire
START/FINISH	Grid reference: SM724252
DOG FRIENDLINESS	One dog-proof stile and farmyard
PARKING	Car park above lifeboat station at St Justinian's
PUBLIC TOILETS	At Porthclais NT car park

This is one of the most rewarding walks, with drop-dead gorgeous coastal scenery and plenty of chances to spot some of Pembrokeshire's varied wildlife. On a calm summer's day, the bobbing boats in Ramsey Sound display the kind of tranquillity you'd usually associate with a Greek island. See it on a rough day, with a spring tide running, and the frothing, seething currents that whip through the narrow channel and it's the opposite. If the views aren't enough, a keen eye and a handy pair of binoculars may well produce sightings of seals, porpoises, dolphins, choughs and even peregrine falcons.

St Justinian was a hermit from Brittany who became the abbot of St Davids Cathedral and acted as St David's confessor. Disillusioned with the lethargic attitude of the monks, he absconded to Ramsey Island to establish a more spiritual community. Some of his more loyal monks travelled with him, but eventually even they became fed up with his strict regimes and chopped off his head. It is said he walked back across Ramsey Sound carrying it in his arms. His remains were buried in the small chapel on the hillside overlooking the sound, which bears his name. Later, St David took them to his own church. St Justinian is revered as a martyr, his assassins are thought to have been under demonic influence, and his life is celebrated on 5 December each year.

Less than 2 miles (3.2km) long and 446ft (136m) high at its tallest point, Ramsey Island is a lumbering humpback ridge separated from the St Davids coast by a narrow sound. Known in Welsh as Ynys Ddewi – St Davids Isle – this is the place where, legend suggests, St David met St Patrick. It's a haven for wildlife and has belonged to the RSPB as a nature reserve since 1992. The eastern coast looks pretty tame, but the western seaboard boasts some of Pembrokeshire's tallest and most impressive cliffs, punctuated with sea caves and rock arches that are the breeding grounds of the area's largest seal colony. At its narrowest point, a string of jagged rocks protrude into the sound, known as The Bitches. Tides gush through the rocks at speeds of up to 8 knots, creating a scene that resembles a mountain river in spate. The resultant waves and eddies make an extreme salt-water playground for white-water kayakers. The island is also populated by a herd of red deer.

Ramsey Sound is one the best places to catch a glimpse of harbour porpoises. Resembling dolphins, though never more than 7ft (2.1m) in length, small schools crop up all around the coast, but are frequently seen feeding in the currents at either end of the sound. Unlike dolphins, they seldom leap from the water, but their arched backs and small dorsal fins are easy to spot as they surface for air. Choose a day when the water is fairly flat, then scan the ocean from a promontory like Pen Dal-Aderyn with a pair of binoculars.

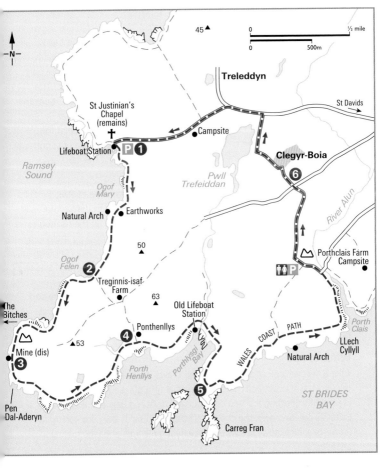

1. Walk down to the lifeboat station and turn left on to the coast path, above the steps. Follow this, passing above a number of lofty, grassy promontories that make great picnic spots. After 0.5 miles (800m), look out for the traces of Iron Age earthworks on the left.

2. Pass a gate and a track on your left – this will be your return route – and swing around to the west above Ogof Felen. This is a good seal pup beach in autumn. The trail climbs slightly and then drops steeply to a ruined copper mine, directly opposite The Bitches.

3. Continue easily to Pen Dal-Aderyn and then swing eastwards to enter St Brides Bay. The path climbs above some magnificent cliffs and passes

between a few rocky outcrops before veering north above the broad bay of Porth Henllys. Drop down into a shallow valley until you come to a fingerpost at a junction of paths.

4. Follow the coast path and then climb up out of the dip. This leads around Maen Llwydwyn and down to Porthlysgi Bay. This was the site of the original St Davids lifeboat station, replaced by the one at St Justinian's. Cross a stream as it runs down the beach and turn left to climb back up, behind the beach, and on to the cliff tops near the rocky island of Carreg Fran.

5. The gradient eases again and the path now cruises comfortably along a wonderful section of coast, studded with rock arches and caves. At Llech Cyllyll, turn back inland to drop down into the deeply cloven inlet of Porth Clais. The harbour was built in the 12th century and was once the main port for St Davids, used for importing coal and timber among other things. The main car park is on the site of the now defunct St Davids gasworks. These in turn had been built over the site of a spring, said to be the place that St David was baptised. Porth Clais is also purported to be the landing place of the legendary magic boar, Twrch Trywyth, after he swam from Ireland to confront King Arthur. Turn left on to the road and climb steeply past the car park. Continue easily to a crossroads.

6. Keep straight ahead to pass Clegyr-Boia and the small lake of Pwll Trefeiddan, a popular stop-over for migrating waterfowl. Turn left at the T-junction and follow the road back to St Justinian's, ignoring the turning to the right.

Where to eat and drink
There are plenty of options in St Davids, but the Pebbles Yard Gallery and Espresso Bar in the centre is probably the best bet for great coffee and freshly prepared food. For pub grub and a drink, the Farmers Arms in Goat Street is a good choice.

What to see
Take a second look at any of the small crows you see as you follow this stretch of coast path. What appears at first glance to be a jackdaw is probably sporting a sharp red bill and bright red legs and is one of Britain's rarest crows, the chough. These small birds are common in Pembrokeshire, however, where they nest on ledges and feed mainly on insects.

While you're there
Take a boat trip around Ramsey Island. As well as getting a close-up look at the seal colonies on the western flanks, you'll also get a great view of the rushing waters of The Bitches. Be sure to wear waterproofs as it can get pretty wet.

THE NORTHERN REACHES OF ST BRIDES BAY

DISTANCE/TIME	9 miles (14.5km) / 4hrs
ASCENT/GRADIENT	1,280ft (390m) / ▲ ▲
PATHS	Coast path
LANDSCAPE	High cliffs and sheltered coves
SUGGESTED MAP	OS Explorer OL35 North Pembrokeshire
START	Grid reference: SM757252
FINISH	Grid reference: SM847224
DOG FRIENDLINESS	Care needed near cliff edges
PARKING	Oriel y Parc car park on Ffordd Cearfai, near tourist information centre
PUBLIC TOILETS	By tourist information centre at start and at Solva harbour

When it comes to coast paths, circular walks are a means to an end, but connoisseurs will always prefer the simplicity of a linear route, especially as there's no need to dilute the quality of the coastal section with often less interesting terrain. The key to success is public transport and fortunately there are a few stretches of the Wales Coastal Path that link well with buses – the county has six separate services shuttling around the coast – to allow some of the finest walks to be completed without compromise. This section, along the northern reaches of St Brides Bay, is one of the best.

Half-way along the walk lies Solva, a village divided into the larger Upper Solva and the more picturesque Lower Solva down by the harbour. It was this harbour that gave Solva its raison d'être and in the Middle Ages the village became a hub for trading in the St Brides Bay area. Solva's well-preserved lime kilns are testament to the harbour's importance as a dropping off point for limestone, which would be heated to produce lime. This would then be spread over the fields to increase fertility. Wool and woollen produce were also traded at the harbour. Indeed, Solva Woollen Mill, a short distance from the village at Middle Mill, claims the crown as the oldest continuously working woollen mill in all of Pembrokeshire. Moved from St Davids to its present location in 1907 by one Tom Griffiths, it was equipped with a 10ft (3m) waterwheel and all the machinery necessary to turn fleeces into useable fabric. The wheel powered a number of looms but there was also a hand loom on site which was used for weaving stair carpet. The mill has been restored in recent years and makes for a fine detour.

A tiny island off Solva, Green Scar – and its even smaller companions Black Scar and The Mare – can be seen for a good deal of the walk. Green Scar is a popular diving spot where an underwater cave can be explored. It is also the scene of a shipwreck. Divers have reported seeing bits of an old boiler protruding from the sands beneath the southern cliffs and a rusting anchor chain.

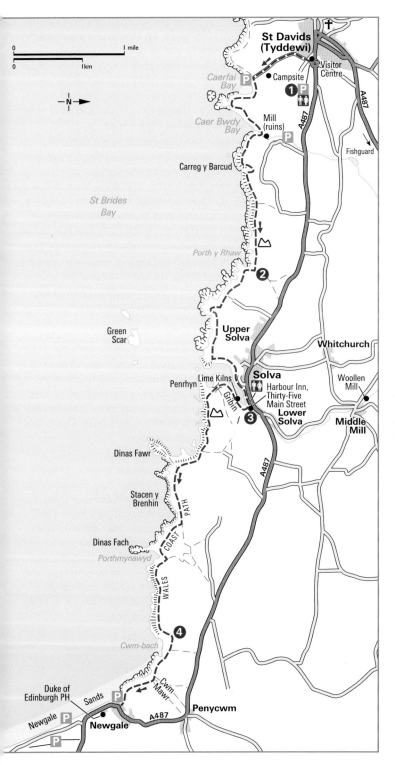

St Davids
(Tyddewi)

Visitor
Centre

Caerfai
Bay

Campsite

A487

Fishguard

Caer Bwdy
Bay

Mill
(ruins)

Carreg y Barcud

St Brides
Bay

Porth y Rhaw

Green
Scar

Upper
Solva

Whitchurch

Solva

Penrhyn

Lime Kilns

Woollen
Mill

Harbour Inn,
Thirty-Five
Main Street

Gribin

Lower
Solva

Middle
Mill

A487

Dinas Fawr

COAST PATH

Stacen y
Brenhin

Dinas Fach

WALES

Porthmynawyd

Cwm-bach

Cwm
Mawr

Duke of
Edinburgh PH

Sands

Newgale

A487

Penycwm

Newgale

0 _____ 1 mile
0 _____ 1 km

N

1. Turn left out of the car park in St Davids and walk down the road towards Caerfai Bay. You'll meet the coast path on the left-hand side of a small car park. Follow it down, ignoring a right turn to the beach, and bear south to round a broad promontory, tipped with a rocky bluff. The path swings left and drops down to Caer Bwdy Bay, where you'll pass a ruined mill on the left. Climb back up on to the cliff tops to continue above Carreg y Barcud and around another inlet. The next section slips by easily, above a series of caves and arches, before you drop steeply down to Porth y Rhaw.

2. Climb out again and enjoy huge views over more cliffs and bluffs. One mile (1.6km) after Porth y Rhaw you'll be drawn back inland as the path dips into the sharp gash of Solva. Go through a gate and follow the field edge down to another gate, where you turn right. This leads on to a narrow track. Follow this down and then around to the left. Continue beneath houses before dropping down a waymarked path on the right that leads down steps to the harbour. Follow the harbour wall along to the Harbour Inn and Thirty-Five Main Street.

3. Cross the bridge and turn left and then right to rejoin the coast path. After taking a right fork to pass above some fantastically well-preserved lime kilns, follow the path up on to the ridge of Gribin. The names Gribin or Cribin literally translate to ridge. At the seaward end you'll pass the banks of an Iron Age settlement. Turn left at a waymarker to drop steeply down steps to a foot-bridge in the valley below. Cross the pebbles at the back of the beach and climb steeply up on to the headland of Penrhyn. Don't be drawn right here but at the top turn, left almost back on yourself to rejoin the cliff edge, a short distance further on. The path continues to climb steadily from this point, passing above a few beautiful beaches before dropping slightly above the pronounced rocky peninsula of Dinas Fawr. An airy scramble along its back makes a great excursion if time allows. Continue easily above Stacen y Brenhin and then drop again into a deep valley by Porthmynawyd. Cross a footbridge and climb the path back on to the cliff tops once more.

4. The wide sweeping sands of Newgale are now visible ahead and, as you are drawn back inland at Cwm-bach, you should be able to see if the tide is low enough to allow you to finish the walk on the beach itself or whether you'll need to climb back up on to the coast path from Cwm Mawr. Climb away from Cwm-bach and then, almost immediately, drop into Cwm Mawr. The beach is accessed by a short scramble down rocks on the right. If the tide's out, continue easily along the beach, past a number of huge caves, to Newgale. Once on Newgale Beach, keep the cliffs to your left and walk up to the huge pebble bank above. Scale this and cross behind the small stream to gain the road. If the tide's too high, climb away from Cwm Mawr and continue along the coast path, with fantastic views west along the coast. This leads out on to the road at Newgale, where you turn right to drop to the village.

Where to eat and drink

The Harbour Inn in Solva and Thirty-Five Main Street café next door are ideally places for a lunch stop. There's also the Duke of Edinburgh pub on the seafront at Newgale.

What to see

The towering cliffs that make up most of this walk provide perfect roosts and nesting ledges for one of Britain's most spectacular birds, the peregrine falcon. These raptors are capable of diving at over 200mph (320kph), and are easily distinguished from kestrels, as they are considerably stockier with a short tail and slate grey uppers. Spring and summer tend to be the best time to see them, as the adult birds are busy finding food for their brood, which when fledged, tend to advertise their spectacular flight practice with a high-pitched kek-kek-kek call.

While you're there

Solva is a pretty little town comprising a cluster of brightly coloured buildings set around an attractive sheltered harbour. As well as boasting a good selection of pubs and restaurants, the main street is home to a number of art galleries, many featuring top-quality seascapes painted by local artists.

A PILGRIMAGE AROUND ST NON'S BAY

DISTANCE/TIME	3.5 miles (5.7km) / 1hr 30min
ASCENT/GRADIENT	262ft (80m) / ▲ ▲
PATHS	Coast path and clear footpaths over farmland
LANDSCAPE	Leafy countryside and dramatic cliffs
SUGGESTED MAP	OS Explorer OL35 North Pembrokeshire
START/FINISH	Grid reference: SM757252
DOG FRIENDLINESS	On lead around St Non's Chapel and St Non's Well
PARKING	Oriel y Parc car park on Ffordd Cearfai, near tourist information centre
PUBLIC TOILETS	Next to tourist information centre and in Porthclais car park

This walk makes a great evening stroll. The paths that lead from the city are pleasant and easy to follow but as always they're quickly forgotten as you step out into the more glamorous surroundings of the coast. The all-too-short section of towering buttresses and jagged islets leads easily to a spot that can claim to be the very heart of spiritual Wales – the birthplace of St David. The serenity of the location soothes the mind in readiness for the short jaunt back to the compact little city he founded.

Considering the immense influence he has had on Welsh culture, little is known about the patron saint himself. His mother is said to be St Non, derived from Nun or Nonita, who was married to a local chieftain called Sant. They settled somewhere near Trwyn Cynddeiriog, the rocky bluff that forms the western walls of the bay named after her. Legend suggests that David was born around AD 500, in the place where the ruined chapel stands today. Although a fierce storm raged throughout his birth, a calm light was said to have lit the scene. By the morning, a fresh spring had erupted near by, becoming the Holy Well of St Non and visited on this walk. St David went on to be baptised by St Elvis at Porthclais, in water from another miraculous spring.

It is believed that David undertook a number of religious odysseys, including one to Jerusalem, before he finally returned to his birthplace around AD 550. He then founded a church and monastery at Glyn Rhosyn, on the banks of the River Alun, on the site of the present cathedral, where he set about trying to spread the Christian word to the, mainly, pagan. St David's Day is celebrated on 1 March every year.

St Davids, with its magnificent cathedral, is a small but wonderful place to visit. Known as Tyddewi – David's House – in Welsh, the city grew as a result of its coastal position at the western extreme of the British mainland. As well as the cathedral and the ruins of the Bishop's Palace, it houses a plethora of gift shops and the Oriel y Parc Gallery and Visitor Centre, close to the car park, is one of the finest in the country.

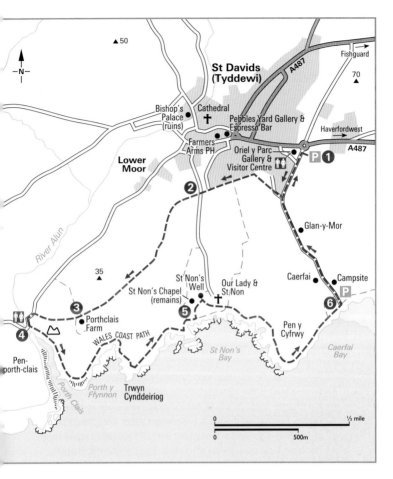

1. Turn left out of the car park and walk down the road, as if you were heading for Caerfai Bay. As the houses thin out, you'll see a turning on the right that leads to more dwellings. Take this turning, and then turn left on to a way-marked bridleway. Follow this bridleway between hedges, past the end of a road and on to reach a junction with another road.

2. Walk straight across and take the waymarked path to a fork, where you keep right to continue to a gate and, a few places later, a second gate. Continue down a path between gorse hedges to a third gate and carry straight on down the left-hand side of a field to a farmyard.

3. Go through the gate and turn left towards the farmyard and then right. As the drive swings left, keep straight ahead with the bank to your right. Continue across the next field and drop down between gorse bushes, keeping straight ahead at a crossroads of paths, to the road at Porthclais. Turn left to the bottom of the valley and then, before crossing the bridge, turn left on to the coast path.

4. Climb up steeply on to the cliff tops, ignoring the path off to the left at the top, and follow the coast path towards Porth y Ffynnon. The next small

headland is Trwyn Cynddeiriog, where there's a lovely grassy platform above the cliffs if you fancy a rest. Continue walking into St Non's Bay and look for a footpath on the left that leads to the ruined chapel.

5. From the chapel, head up to a gate that leads to St Non's Well and, from there, follow the path beneath the new chapel and straight ahead on to the coast path. Turn left to climb easily on to Pen y Cyfrwy, continue around this and drop down towards Caerfai Bay.

6. You'll eventually come out beneath the Caerfai Bay car park where you turn left and climb some steps. Go through the entrance of the car park onto the road, which you follow back to St Davids and the start of the walk.

Where to eat and drink

Apart from the tiny seasonal café in the car park at Porthclais, the best bet for refreshment is St Davids where there's plenty of choice. A favourite pub is the Farmers Arms on Goat Street, which has a good garden and serves up all the usual pub fare. For non-alcoholic refreshment, try the excellent Pebbles Yard Gallery and Espresso Bar.

What to see

Shortly after the stiff climb out of Porthclais, you'll round Trwyn Cynddeiriog, the headland that divides Porth y Ffynnon from St Non's Bay. This is where St Non and Sant, St David's parents, were said to have lived. A short distance further along the coast path, at the head of the bay, you'll see a footpath on the left that leads to the ruined chapel. This is thought to have been built in the 13th century on the spot where St David was born. A path then leads to a gate, behind which you'll see St Non's Well and a grotto. Further up the hill is the newer chapel, dedicated to Our Lady and St Non. This was actually built in the 1930s using stone from other principle local evangelical sites, including the original chapel.

While you're there

St Davids Cathedral is both architecturally stunning and spiritually moving. In 1120 Pope Calixtus II decreed that two pilgrimages to St Davids were the equivalent of one to Rome – an honour indeed. The cathedral and the nearby Bishop's Palace play host to a series of classical concerts every summer.

BROAD HAVEN AND THE HAROLDSTON WOODS

DISTANCE/TIME	3.5 miles (5.7km) / 1hr 30min
ASCENT/GRADIENT	290ft (88m) / ▲
PATHS	Woodland trail, country lanes and coast path
LANDSCAPE	Mixed woodland and lofty cliffs above broad beach
SUGGESTED MAP	OS Explorer OL36 South Pembrokeshire
START/FINISH	Grid reference: SM863140
DOG FRIENDLINESS	Poop scoop around car park and beach, care needed on cliff tops
PARKING	Car park in Broad Haven
PUBLIC TOILETS	Between car park and beach

Woodland walking is something of a rarity along the Wales Coastal Path, so this short stretch of permissive path, which sneaks through a narrow strip of woodland separating Broad Haven from Haroldston, makes a refreshing diversion from the usual salty air and the cries of the seabirds. This is the easiest of the Pembrokeshire walks in the book, with an almost billiard table-level section of coast path, some of which has been surfaced for access by wheelchair users. The artificial path, however, takes nothing away from the quality of the scenery, which is magnificent.

The cliffs here are of softer shales and millstone grit making them prone to erosion and subsidence, as you'll witness first-hand along the way. Amazingly, this whole stretch of coast sits on top of huge coal reserves, but the last colliery, which was situated further north in Nolton Haven, actually closed down in the early 1900s. As you progress south, you'll pass the crumpled remains of an Iron Age fort on Black Point and also a diminutive standing stone, known as the Harold Stone, which is tucked away in a field on the left as you approach Broad Haven. It's said to mark the spot where Harold, the Earl of Wessex, defeated the Welsh in the 11th century, but it's actually more likely to be Bronze Age.

Broad Haven is about as close as you'll get to a traditional seaside resort in north Pembrokeshire. The town's popularity as a holiday destination blossomed in the early 1800s, but recent years have seen an acceleration in development that has resulted in almost wall-to-wall caravan parks and a significant rise in the number of residential properties. The beach is beautiful, with gently sloping sands encased in brooding dark cliffs. As well as the usual selection of family holiday-makers, it's a popular place with windsurfers. This is due partly to shops and places to eat behind the beach, and because the prevalent southwesterlies that blow across and onshore from the left make it a safe but fun place to play in the sometimes sizeable surf.

At low tide, it's possible to walk south along the beach to the charming village of Little Haven. A walk northwards will reveal some fascinating rock formations beneath the headland. These include Den's Door, an impressive double arch in a rugged sea stack; the Sleek Stone, a humpback rock forced into its contorted position by a geological fault; and Shag Rock and Emmet Rock. Contorted layers of rock are also clearly visible in the main cliffs.

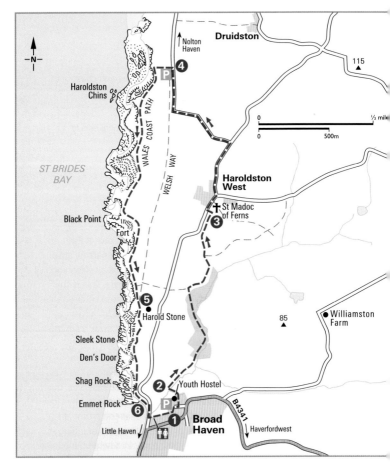

1. From anywhere in the car park, walk towards the youth hostel and follow a waymarked path marked Coedwig Haroldston Woods that runs between the hostel and the former coastguard building, now a holiday let. Fork left at the junction with the holiday park path and continue to a gate then a kissing gate, to continue with the stream on your left.

2. Cross the stream by a bridge and now, with the valley floor to your right, go through a gate and bear left to continue easily upwards until you reach a T-junction of paths by a fingerpost. Turn right here, past a part-concealed bench on the right, and then swing left to continue upwards to another junction of paths by a small chapel, St Madoc of Ferns.

3. Turn left to the road and then right on to it to walk uphill, with the church on your right. Ignore the turning to the right, then take the first left, towards Druidston Haven. Follow this past an ineffectual cattle grid to a sharp

right-hand bend. Continue for another 300yds (274m) to the Haroldston Chins parking area and a gate on the left.

4. Go through the gate and follow the well-surfaced track down towards the coast. On reaching the cliff tops, bear around to the left and continue past Black Point.

5. After passing the Harold Stone situated in front of a modern white house on your left, fork right through a gate to remain on the coast path (marked with an acorn). The path starts to drop, generally quite easily, but there is one steep step. Follow the path down to meet the road and turn right.

6. Cross over the bridge and then, just before the road you are on merges into the main road, turn left on to a tarmac footpath that leads through a green and back to the car park.

Where to eat and drink
There's plenty of choice, including pubs, cafés and chip shops in Broad Haven, but the top place for atmosphere, food and setting has to be The Swan Inn on the tiny harbourside in Little Haven. It's an intimate little pub ideal for lunch, dinner or just a pint on the sea wall.

What to see
As you turn the sharp right-hand bend on the road at Point 3, you'll see a good track running parallel to the road in the field on your left. This is an ancient trade route, known as the Welsh Way, that runs from Monk's Haven – more commonly known as St Ishmael's – to Whitesands Beach. It was considered a safer mode of transport than sailing across the waters of the bay.

While you're there
For a memorable sunset experience, head a few miles north to the tiny beach at Nolton Haven, where you can enjoy the fading daylight in a truly atmospheric setting. A short walk north along the coast path from the beach leads to the distinctive pillar of Rickets Head, which is also easily visible from the beach at Newgale.

VIEWS FROM THE MARLOES PENINUSLA

DISTANCE/TIME	6 miles (9.7km) / 2hrs 30min
ASCENT/GRADIENT	420ft (128m) / ▲ ▲
PATHS	Coast path and clear footpaths, short section on tarmac
LANDSCAPE	Rugged cliff tops and beautiful sandy beaches
SUGGESTED MAP	OS Explorer OL36 South Pembrokeshire
START/FINISH	Grid reference: SM761089
DOG FRIENDLINESS	Care near cliff tops and poop scoop on beaches
PARKING	National Trust car park above Martin's Haven, near Marloes village
PUBLIC TOILETS	Marloes village and near information centre at start of walk

The Marloes Peninsula forms the westernmost tip of the southern shores of St Brides Bay. The paddle-shaped headland is a popular place to walk due to the narrow neck that affords minimum inland walking for maximum time spent on the coast. It is famous for its stunning scenery, which includes two of the National Park's finest and least-crowded beaches, some secluded coves that are often inhabited by seals, and wonderfully rugged coastline. There are also fine views over a narrow but turbulent sound to the small islands of Skomer and Skokholm – two significant seabird breeding grounds. The walking is captivating, even by Pembrokeshire standards.

Skomer is the largest of the Pembrokeshire islands and is one of the most significant wildlife habitats in the whole country. The island, separated from the mainland by the rushing waters of Jack Sound, measures approximately 1.5 miles (2.4km) from north to south and 2 miles (3.2km) from east to west. It was declared a National Nature Reserve in 1959 and, as well as the protection it receives as part of the National Park, it's also designated as a Site of Special Scientific Interest (SSSI), a Special Protection Area (SPA) and a Geological Conservation Review Site (GCR). Much of the land is a Scheduled Ancient Monument, courtesy of a number of clearly visible Iron Age settlements and enclosures. And to put the icing on the cake, the sea that surrounds the island is a Marine Nature Reserve, one of only three in the United Kingdom; the others are Lundy, off the North Devon coast and Strangford Lough in Northern Ireland.

The two stars of the Skomer show are the diminutive but colourful puffin and the dowdy and secretive Manx shearwater. Puffins need little introduction; their colourful beaks and clown-like facial markings put them high on everybody's list of favourite birds. They arrive in April and lay a single egg in a burrow. The chick hatches at the end of May and the adult birds spend the next two months ferrying back catches of sand eels for their flightless offspring. After around seven weeks of this lavish attention, the chick leaves the nest, usually at night, and makes its way to the sea. It will spend the next few years at sea, only returning when it reaches breeding maturity. Between April and July, there are more than 42,500 puffins on the island.

The mouse-like shearwater is slightly larger than the puffin but it also lays its single egg in a burrow, overlooking the sea. It may not be as obviously endearing as its painted neighbour, especially as most visitors to the island never actually see one, but it's a beautiful and fascinating bird in its own right and there are in fact around 150,000 pairs on Skomer, Skokholm and Middleholm; which amounts to about 60 per cent of the world's total population. The reason they are seldom seen is because they are fairly vulnerable to predators on land so they leave the nest at dawn and spend the whole day at sea, not returning to their burrow until it's almost dark. A careful seawatch at last light may reveal them gathering in huge rafts just offshore or even endless lines of flying birds returning to the island – against the sunset, it's quite a magical sight.

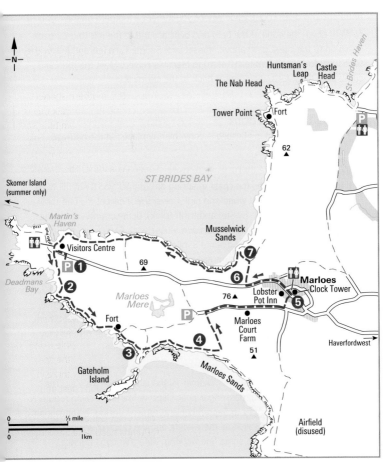

1. From the bottom of the car park, walk down to the bottom of the hill. Bear around to the left, then go through the gate straight ahead into the Deer Park. Turn left and follow the path along to a gate and out on to the coast.

2. With the sea to your right, continue easily along over Deadman's Bay. The next section cruises along easily, passing the earthworks of an Iron Age fort on the left as you approach Gateholm Island.

3. It is possible to get across to the island at low tide, but care is needed to scramble over the slippery rocks. To continue the walk, follow the coast path, above the western end of the beautiful Marloes Sands until you drop almost onto the beach. Turn left along the wide well-made gravel path.

4. Climb up to the road; turn right here. Follow the road along for around 0.75 miles (1.2km) to a hedged bridleway on the left. Follow this down and emerge by the clock tower.

5. Turn left and pass the Lobster Pot Inn, continuing ahead to leave the village. Ignore a few tracks on the right, as the road bends around to the left, and continue out into open countryside where you'll meet a footpath on the right.

6. Walk down the edge of the field and bear around to the left to drop back down on to the coast path above Musselwick Sands. Turn left and follow the path west for over 1.5 miles (2.4km) to Martin's Haven. Meet the road and climb past the information centre back to the car park.

Where to eat and drink

The Lobster Pot Inn in Marloes is conveniently placed at the half-way point of the walk.

What to see

If you're walking along the coast in spring or summer you'll not fail to be impressed by the small white and pink flowers that carpet the cliff tops. These are sea campion (white) and thrift (pink), both common along the Pembrokeshire coast. As you approach Musselwick Sands, you should be able to see a small island some 8 miles (12.9km) offshore. This is Grassholm and during the summer months it appears almost pure white. It isn't due to the colour of the rock but thousands of breeding pairs of gannets that return to the island every year. Unlike the puffins and shearwaters of Skomer, the gannets are easily spotted, usually in small flocks, cruising a few hundred yards out looking for fish. If you spot them, watch closely and you'll probably witness their spectacular dive as they fold in their wings and plummet like darts into the water.

While you're there

If you have a day to spare then Skomer Island is well worth a visit. The Dale Princess, a 50-seat passenger boat, departs Martin's Haven regularly every morning from April to September and returns during the afternoon except on Mondays. As well as the wildlife and the relics of ancient civilisations, there's also some fine walking. Note that dogs are not allowed on the island.

A CIRCUIT OF ST ANN'S HEAD

DISTANCE/TIME	6 miles (9.7km) / 3hrs
ASCENT/GRADIENT	590ft (180m) / ▲ ▲
PATHS	Coast path, clear paths across farmland, many stiles
LANDSCAPE	Dramatic coastline and entrance to Milford Haven
SUGGESTED MAP	OS Explorer OL36 South Pembrokeshire
START/FINISH	Grid reference: SM811058
DOG FRIENDLINESS	Care needed near livestock
PARKING	Large car park next to beach in Dale
PUBLIC TOILETS	At start

Despite its beauty and excellence as a walking venue, St Ann's Head is most famous for an event that reads as a sombre tale of incompetence. The precarious balance between the region's oil refinery and the fragile ecosystems of some of Britain's finest coastline was destroyed on 15 February 1996, when the Sea Empress oil tanker grounded on rocks just off St Ann's Head. The collision wasn't particularly bad and because it had taken place near low tide, the ship could have been quickly recovered had the right systems been in place. Tragically, the recovery became a comedy of errors. Numerous realistic salvage propositions were refused and, though the fated ship still had working engines, at one stage she was allegedly denied permission to continue into port under her own steam. By the Sunday evening she was still stranded, having lost only 2,000 tonnes of her cargo. High winds and strong tides continued to batter her against the rocks and finally, six days after she first grounded, she limped into the Haven having spilt at least 72,000 tonnes. The effects were catastrophic: huge oil slicks hit 175 miles (280km) of coastline, including the National Park, 35 Sites of Special Scientific Interest and a National Maritime Nature Reserve.

The immediate victims were the birds: 6,900 were recovered either dead or rescued, but it is estimated that over 20,000 died. The species worst hit was a small black duck known as the common scoter. The damage to fish stocks and other marine life will take years to gauge accurately. The tourist industry was temporarily devastated and the full effect on fishing and related trades won't be known for decades.

The one course of action that won't be undertaken to avoid the repeat of such a disaster is the building of a lighthouse off St Ann's Head. That's because there already is one. The original lighthouse here was built in 1714 while the current one first shed a light on the seas in 1841. This route takes you right past it and the row of cottages once used to house the lighthouse keepers and their families.

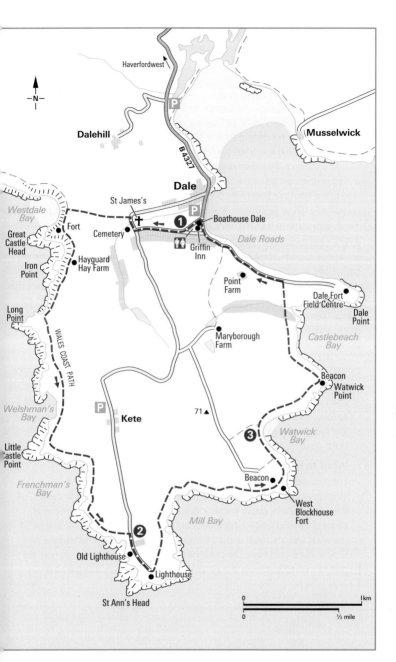

1. Walk back onto the sea front and turn right and then bear right along the road, to head away from the water and between houses. Continue to a T-junction where you turn right, and then as the road bends right again, bear left, through a gate on to a track. As the track bears left, keep ahead and follow the footpath up through a field to a gate that leads on to the coast path above the quiet surfing beach of Westdale Bay. Turn left and climb the steps up on to

Great Castle Head, occupied by an Iron Age fort. For the next 2 miles (3.2km), continue along the coast path with the sea to your right and farmland to your left. Despite the spectacular scenery, there are no real drops or climbs and no real opportunities to get lost.

2. When you meet the road, turn right and walk along the drive, past the old lighthouse, now a private residence, to a gate. Here, the coast path veers left and then immediately right, to follow a series of marker posts along a fence towards the lighthouse and a bank of cottages on the right. At the cottages, bear left then turn sharp left to cross the green to a track that leads behind a walled enclosure. This then drops to join the coast again above Mill Bay, where a plaque gives details of the landing of the exiled Henry Tudor in 1485, on his way to the Battle of Bosworth. Descend to cross the head of the bay and climb up again to follow field edges around to the beacon on West Blockhouse Point. You'll then come to a crossroads, where you keep straight ahead.

3. The path continues to follow the coast, passing the finest of the beaches along this stretch, Watwick Bay. Continue away from the beach and follow the path, both on cliff tops and field edges, and past a dew pond, to the beacon on Watwick Point. After running along the edge of another two fields, you start the descent to Castlebeach. Cross the footbridge and climb up steps towards the narrow peninsula of Dale Point. As the ground levels, you'll meet a junction of paths where you keep straight ahead to the road. Turn left and follow it down, through woodland, to Dale and the car park.

Where to eat and drink

The waterfront Griffin Inn in Dale is a local institution usually bustling with sailors, surfers, divers and a whole host of other outdoor enthusiasts. The food and drink are as good as the atmosphere. Alternatively try The Boathouse Dale, which has a large outdoor seating area.

What to see

The blockhouses and fort along this stretch of coast show how much strategic military importance was placed on Milford Haven in the past. West Blockhouse, above Watwick Bay, was built in 1857 for a garrison of 80 men. Dale Fort, now a field study centre and seen towards the end of the walk, was also built in the 1850s and would have been garrisoned by a similar number of men. The beacons that dominate the headlands now are part of a complex series of waymarkers that aid tankers into the Haven.

AROUND MILFORD HAVEN

DISTANCE/TIME	9 miles (14.5km) / 4hrs
ASCENT/GRADIENT	1,017ft (310m) / ▲ ▲
PATHS	Coast path and easy tracks over agricultural land, short road section, many stiles
LANDSCAPE	Rugged coastline, magnificent beach and sheltered harbour
SUGGESTED MAP	OS Explorer OL36 South Pembrokeshire
START/FINISH	Grid reference: SM854031
DOG FRIENDLINESS	Care needed on cliff tops and near livestock
PARKING	Car park at West Angle Bay
PUBLIC TOILETS	West Angle Bay

The narrow finger of land that juts out between Freshwater West and Angle Bay forms the eastern wall of the mouth of Milford Haven. On the northern edge of the peninsula, the waters are passive, lapping against a coastline that's gentle and sloping, but as you round the headland, a radical transformation takes place. Here, the cliffs stand tall and proud, defiantly resisting the full brunt of the considerable Atlantic swells. There are other differences too. While the views along the seaward coast are wild and unspoilt, the inner shores of the Haven reveal the smoking oil refinery chimneys that dominate the eastern skyline.

The narrow-necked shape of the peninsula lends itself to a challenging circular walk that shows both sides of the coin. The outward leg, as far as the sweeping sands of Freshwater West, is about as tough as coast path walking gets; constantly dipping and climbing on narrow, often quite exposed, paths. The return leg is a little more civilised, tracking easily around the curve of Angle Bay and following field edges back out on to the headland.

Milford Haven is the name of both a huge natural inlet, once described by Admiral Nelson as 'the finest port in Christendom', and the small town that nestles on its northern shores. Despite the obvious advantages of the sheltered waterways, the Haven saw only limited development until the 20th century. Although there is evidence of earlier settlements and shipping activity, the town, as it is now, and original dock, sprang up in the late 1700s to house a small whaling community that had fled from Nantucket, Massachusetts, during the American War of Independence. Despite interest from the military, which saw the potential for shipbuilding, lack of funding at the time prohibited serious expansion. Various enterprising ideas followed over the ensuing years, but by the end of the 19th century, the whaling had all but declined and the Navy had moved to nearby Pembroke Dock.

Large-scale fishing in the rich waters of the Pembrokeshire coast threw the port a lifeline in the early 1900s and then, as this too declined, mainly due to over-fishing and the related smaller catches, energy production took over as the area's main industry. There were once three refineries and a power station at the head of the Haven. One of the refineries has now closed and the original oil-fired power station was also closed after public pressure against its plan to burn a controversial fuel type. A LNG (Liquified Natural Gas) and Pembroke B, a gas-fired power station were both opened in the early years of the 21st century and both are currently the largest such facilities of their type, in Europe.

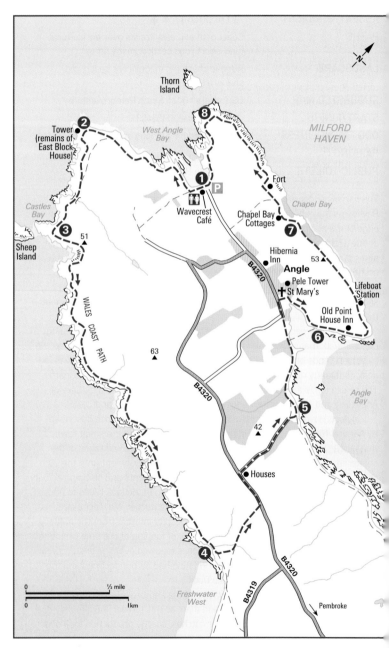

1. Facing the sea, walk left out of the car park and pass between the Wavecrest café and the toilets to a waymarked gate. Follow the field edge, passing through further gates, and eventually leading out on to the coast, where a right fork drops to a ruined tower on a slender headland.

2. Continue back up from this, pass through further gates and then go down to a little footbridge. Climb up from this and pass Sheep Island on your right.

3. Continue along the coast, dropping steeply into a succession of valleys and climbing back up each time. As you reach the northern end of Freshwater West, keep your eye open for a footpath waymarker to the left.

4. Cross a stile and walk up the floor of the valley, swinging left to a stile at the top. Cross the next field, to a kissing gate and another field to a stile. Cross this and turn left on to the road and walk past a cluster of houses to a right-hand turn. Follow this all the way down to the coast and turn left on to the coast path to merge on to a drive.

5. Take the drive to a bridleway sign on the right. If the tide is low, you can cross the estuary here and continue along the bank of pebbles to the road on the other side. If it's not, carry on along the drive to join a road that leads into Angle village and turn right by the church to follow a gravel track over a bridge and around to the right.

6. Continue around, pass the Old Point House Inn on your left and follow field edges to the gravel turning point above the lifeboat station on your right. Keep straight ahead and continue through a succession of fields into a wooded area.

7. You'll join a broad track that runs around Chapel Bay cottages and fort. Keep straight ahead to follow the narrow path back above the coast. This eventually rounds the headland by Thorn Island.

8. As you descend into West Angle Bay, the path diverts briefly into a field to avoid a landslide. Continue downwards and bear right on to a drive that drops you back to the car park.

Where to eat and drink

The Hibernia Inn in Angle village is conveniently placed for lunch or a drink, but you'd do even better to hold on for the stunningly positioned Old Point House Inn, as you climb above Angle Bay and back out on to the headland. Alternatively the Wavecrest Café serves hot and cold drinks and a range of tasty snacks from sandwiches and paninis to jacket potatoes.

What to see

Milford Haven's potential vulnerability to invasion has led to considerable defences being constructed around its entrance. The stone blockhouse on Thorn Island, now a hotel, is testament to this, as are the other fortifications on St Ann's Head.

While you're there

Take a drive or, better still, a walk across the magnificent Cleddau bridge that spans the estuary between Neyland and Pembroke Dock. The sweeping curve of the lofty 1970s construction provides stunning views over the whole haven and the coast beyond.

BEACHES AND LAKES AT STACKPOLE

DISTANCE/TIME	6 miles (9.7km) / 2hrs 30min
ASCENT/GRADIENT	390ft (119m) / ▲
PATHS	Easy coast path, quiet lanes and well-trodden waterside walkways
LANDSCAPE	Magnificent limestone headlands, secluded beaches and tranquil waterways
SUGGESTED MAP	OS Explorer OL36 South Pembrokeshire
START/FINISH	Grid reference: SR976938
DOG FRIENDLINESS	Care needed on cliff tops and near livestock
PARKING	National Trust car park above Broad Haven Beach
PUBLIC TOILETS	At start and at Stackpole Quay

The limestone headlands of St Govan's and Stackpole make up some of the most impressive coastline in south Pembrokeshire. Their grass-covered, plateau-like tops are very different to the relentlessly undulating ground covered by most of the coast path and, as a result, an excursion around this most southerly point of Pembrokeshire is surprisingly relaxing. The cliffs, however, make up only a short section of a varied walk that crosses two of the region's finest beaches and also explores some beautiful inland waters. Broad Haven is often referred to as Broad Haven South, to avoid confusion with the town and beach of the same name in St Brides Bay.

The beach here is a broad gem of white sand, backed by rolling dunes and flanked by impressive headlands. Barafundle Bay is equally as picturesque, but also benefits from a lack of road access that keeps it relatively quiet for most of the year. The final attraction of this simple circuit is the three-fingered waterway that probes deeply inland from Broad Haven. The wooded shores and mirror-calm waters make a refreshing change and a lovely contrast to the wildness of the coast.

The cliffs between Linney Head, closed to the public as part of the MOD firing range, and Stackpole Head, which is visited on this walk, are made up of carboniferous limestone and comprise some of the best limestone coastal scenery in Britain. Exposed to the full force of the Atlantic at their feet, they are often overhanging and also contain many caves and blowholes. A few spectacular sea stacks have survived the battering and now stud the coast a short distance offshore – Church Rock, seen on this walk, just off Broad Haven Beach, is one of the finest examples. The area is also one of the most popular rock climbing locations in the country.

This series of interconnecting lakes was created at the turn of the 19th-century by Baron Cawdor, once the owner of the Stackpole Estate. He dammed a small tidal creek, which then flooded the three tributary valleys. Subsequent drifting of sand has created a large marram grass-covered dune system behind the beach. The lakes are rich in wildlife, with herons prowling the shallows, swans, ducks, moorhens and coots all visible on the surface, and shyer creatures such as kingfishers often spotted. The Lily Ponds are managed as a National Nature Reserve, and the lilies themselves are at their best in June, while the woodland is a magnificent spectacle in spring and autumn.

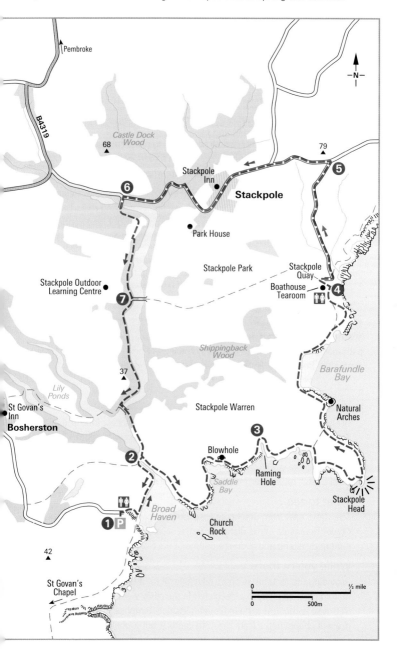

1. From the car park, head back to the National Trust building at the head of the lane and bear right, down a tarmac path and a set of steps, to the beach. Cross the beach and keep left to walk up the creek to a footbridge.

2. Go over the footbridge and turn left then shortly afterwards turn right at a fingerpost marked Stackpole Quay. Walk above rocky outcrops, above the beach, to a gate. Follow the grassy path around the headland and back inland to a gate above Saddle Bay. Continue around a large blowhole and up to a gate above a deeply cloven zawn (inlet), known as the Raming Hole.

3. Go through a gate a few hundred yards later and hug the coastline on your right to walk around Stackpole Head. As you turn back inland, pass a blowhole and then go through a gate to drop down to Barafundle Bay. Cross the back of the beach and climb up the steps on the other side to an archway in the wall. Continue through a gate and down some steps to Stackpole Quay.

4. Turn left, above the tiny harbour, and drop to pass the Boathouse Café on your left before turning sharp right on to a road. Follow this past some buildings on the right and up to a T-junction, where you turn left.

5. From here to Point 6 there is no pavement so care should be taken as vehicles can approach quickly along this section of winding road. Drop down into Stackpole village, pass the Stackpole Inn on the right, and continue around a series of bends until you come to a road on the left, over a bridge.

6. Cross the bridge and turn left to follow a good path along the side of the lake. Continue along this, ignoring a path off to the right, and turn left at a T-junction next to a building. Carry on along the lakeside to a bridge.

7. Don't cross the bridge, but drop down on to a narrow path that keeps straight ahead and follow it with the lake on your left. Continue ahead to another bridge, cross it, then carry on with the lake now on your right. This path leads to the footbridge that you crossed at Point 2. Retrace your steps across the beach and up the steps back to the car park.

Where to eat and drink

St Govan's Inn at Bosherston is a hidden gem, with great food and a selection of real ales. The walls are often decorated with photographs of climbers in seemingly impossible positions on local cliffs. Dogs are allowed in the stable bar at the back. The Boathouse tea room is open from Easter to October for snacks, drinks and meals.

What to see

The views east from Stackpole Head stretch from Caldey Island to the Gower Peninsula in the distance. To the south, you may be able to make out Lundy Island and even the outline of the North Devon coast.

While you're there

Providing the footpath is open, take a stroll to St Govan's Chapel, a stone building tucked away in a deep cleft in the cliffs, west of St Govan's Head. St Govan is thought to have been an Irish contemporary of St David. The present chapel dates from the 13th century, but probably incorporates some much older stonework.

MANORBIER AND SWANLAKE BAY

DISTANCE/TIME	5 miles (8km) / 1hr 30min
ASCENT/GRADIENT	935ft (285m) / ▲ ▲
PATHS	Coast path, clear paths across farmland
LANDSCAPE	Sandy coves and dramatic coastline
SUGGESTED MAP	OS Explorer OL36 South Pembrokeshire
START/FINISH	Grid reference: SS063976
DOG FRIENDLINESS	Difficult stiles, poop scoop on beaches; keep on lead and off grass near house on The Dak
PARKING	Pay-and-display car park below the castle
PUBLIC TOILETS	In the car park at the start of the walk

This is a delightful walk that runs along the heads of some magnificent cliffs and visits a wonderful and remote sandy cove. The outward leg isn't particularly inspirational, but the narrow lane provides convenient access to the highest ground and the section across farmland is open and breezy, with fine views over the coast. Once reached, the narrow belt of white sand that makes up Swanlake Bay provides ample reward for your efforts. Flanked on both sides by impressive sandstone crags and cut off from easy road access by the farmland that you've just traversed, it sees few visitors and provides a stunning setting for a picnic.

Once lauded by its most famous son, Giraldus Cambrensis, alias Gerald of Wales, as the 'pleasantest spot in Wales'. Giraldus was born Gerald de Barri, the grandson of Odo, the first Norman Lord of the Manor, in 1146. Manorbier these days is best described as an attractive but sleepy coastal village dominated by a mighty castle and set among some of south Pembrokeshire's prettiest and most unspoilt countryside.

The village name derives from 'Maenor of Pyrrus' or 'Manor of Pyr'. Pyrrus was the first Celtic abbot of Caldey, a nearby island first inhabited by monks in the 6th century AD and known in Welsh as Ynys Byr, or Pyro's Island. Its landscape is wild and unspoilt and its buildings are inspirationally simple. There is a working Benedictine monastery and a number of ornate churches, including 12th-century St Illtyd's, with its ancient sandstone cross.

Despite the profusion of well-preserved castles in this corner of the world, it still comes as a surprise to discover such an impressive edifice tucked away in this tiny village. The original castle stems from the late 11th century, but the stone building that stands tall and proud over the beach and village these days was constructed in the early 12th century.

The castle is privately owned, but open to the public for tours. As well as the splendid views over the bay from the top of the castle walls, you'll also see many stately rooms, occupied these days by waxwork models of various figures, including Gerald, hard at work on his accounts.

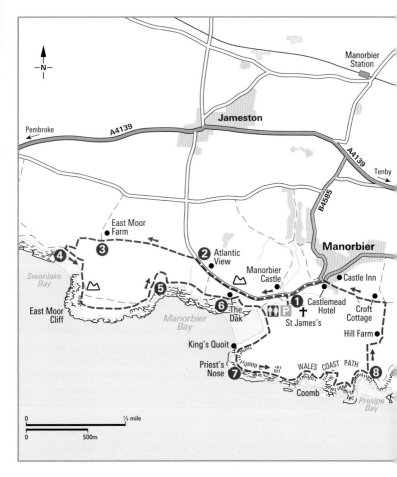

1. Walk out of the car park entrance and turn left towards the sea. Stay on the road as it bears around to the right and climbs steeply above the coast. Pass the impressively situated and well-named Atlantic View cottage on your right before reaching a double gate on your left.

2. Go through the gate and walk along the field edge, with a bank and fence on your right, to reach a gate. Go through this and continue heading in the same direction to a gate close to the farm which you also pass through. Continue to a kissing gate by the farmhouse, which brings you into a small enclosure, then to another kissing gate that leads you away from the buildings.

3. Continue again along the edge of the field to another kissing gate. Go through and turn left to drop down the field edge to a zig-zag that leads on to the coast path. Access to the beach is more or less directly beneath you.

4. Turn left on to the coast path and go through a gate and steeply uphill. You'll eventually reach the top on a lovely airy ridge that swings east and then north to drop steeply down into a narrow dip above Manorbier Bay.

5. Climb out of the dip to a gate and continue walking easily above the rocky beach. This path leads to a drive, beneath a large house, The Dak.

6. Continue beneath The Dak and uphill slightly to a gate, where the coast path drops off to the right. Follow this as it skirts a small car park and then winds down through the gorse and bracken to the beach. Cross the stream and cross the back of the beach to a set of steps that lead up to the coast path. Climb up through the bracken on a narrow path that shortly passes the impressive King's Quoit, a Stone Age burial chamber with a 16ft (4.8m) capstone supported by two smaller stones.

7. With fine views over Manorbier Beach and the sandstone headland, continue up to the apex of the Priest's Nose, another sandstone headland with a number of caves. The path now passes close to a series of deeply cloven zawns (inlets), then turns east to carve a narrow walkway across the steep hillside. The trail turns inland again to round a steep-sided valley. Climb away from this and continue back out on to the headland to reach Presipe Bay.

8. At a gate bearing a notice about the nearby air defence range turn left, away from the coast, to walk up the edge of the field. Continue through a gate to a waymarker pointing you right towards Hill Farm and to a point where it swings hard left. Skirt around the farm and go straight ahead to meet a surfaced drive. Turn left to pass Croft Cottage and continue to a T-junction where you bear right. Follow this to the road, by the Castlemead Hotel. Turn left to walk down the road, back to the car park.

Where to eat and drink
The Castle Inn, in the centre of Manorbier, is a cosy and friendly place with a good selection of food and a decent choice of ales. It has a great garden where you can sit and relax after a hard morning or afternoon's walk.

What to see
The cliffs along this part of the coast show some dramatic irregularities in the old red sandstone that forms them. East Moor Cliff, the eastern headland of Swanlake Bay, is a prime example, with huge blocks creating impressive bastions. There are a few low-grade rock climbs on the cliff, which is huge and split by a very deep fissure.

While you're there
Tenby is the unofficial tourism capital of south Pembrokeshire and although its crowded streets and rows of hotels and B&Bs come as something of a shock after the more rural spots along the coast, it's still a charming, mainly Georgian, town with a beautiful harbour and plenty of attractions to keep you busy on a rainy day. Of particular historical interest are the original town walls. They were so effective that the Norman castle was made pretty much redundant.

LAUGHARNE:
A CIRCULAR STROLL

DISTANCE/TIME	5.5 miles (8.8km) / 2hrs 30min
ASCENT/GRADIENT	900ft (270m) / ▲
PATHS	Well-marked paths and tracks, some of which may be muddy in winter; a number of stiles
LANDSCAPE	Woods, fields, town, salt marsh, estuary views
SUGGESTED MAP	OS Explorer 177 Carmarthen & Kidwelly
START/FINISH	Grid reference: SN301106
DOG FRIENDLINESS	Livestock in fields – dogs on lead throughout
PARKING	Car park below Laugharne Castle
PUBLIC TOILETS	By the castle near the start of the walk (small charge)
NOTES	During exceptionally high tides, the car park in Laugharne is prone to flooding – see information board for details

The quirky little town of Laugharne has found fame the world over for its association with the poet Dylan Thomas. Dylan lived in Laugharne for a total of seven years – between 1938 and 1941 and then from 1949 to his death in 1953 – but always regarded the town as a kind of spiritual home. There is no doubt that he revelled in the town's reputation for eccentricity, exaggerating its peculiarities in the fictional Llareggub ('bugger-all' backwards) of *Under Milk Wood*. A different kind of influence, more melancholic and introspective, is evident in later poems such as 'Poem in October', 'Poem on his Birthday' and the elegiac 'Over Sir John's Hill' – all imbued with the town's distinctive atmosphere and landscape.

One of Thomas's favourite Laugharne walks was a path across a steep, wooded shoulder of Sir John's Hill, high above the Taf Estuary. Known locally as the 'New Walk', the path provided access to valuable cockle beds on the mudflats near Salt House Farm, but it was its scenic qualities that Dylan appreciated. A journey along the path is the inspiring conceit behind 'Poem in October', which describes an ascent of Sir John's Hill on the poet's 'thirtieth year to heaven'.

Later in the walk, you will pass St Martin's Church, where Dylan and his wife Caitlin are buried in the new cemetery, and the Boathouse, Dylan's home for his final four years. The Boathouse, described in 'Poem on his Birthday' as 'his house on stilts', is a museum dedicated to the writer's life and work, and nearby is his writing shed where several great works were penned. There are great views across the tidal estuary.

But there is more to Laugharne than Dylan Thomas. At the centre of the town's distinct identity is its unique corporation – the only medieval corporation still in existence in the UK. Founded in 1291 by local Norman lord Guy de Brian, the corporation invested its burgesses (who were mainly

English) with a range of special privileges to ensure their loyalty against the Welsh. As a result, Laugharne has remained a predominantly English-speaking town. Today, the corporation maintains some of Laugharne's more colourful traditions. These include the Laugharne Common Walk, which occurs every three years on Whit Monday. Led by the Portreeve (the leader of the corporation, appointed annually), this all-day walk is a variation on the medieval tradition of 'beating the bounds', retracing and thereby reaffirming the town's ancient boundaries.

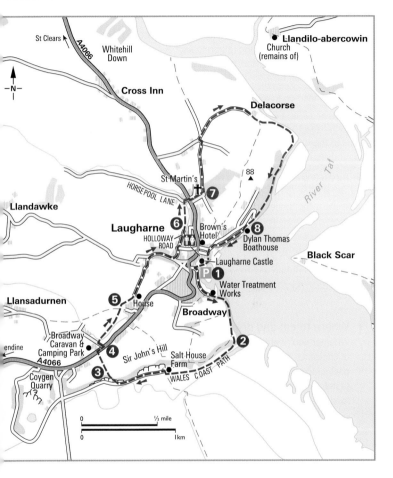

1. From the car park, follow a tarmac track away from the castle. Just before the water treatment works, bear right on to a gravel path ('Dylan's Birthday Walk'). Climb steeply through woodland to a path junction by a bench and information board. Take the left-hand fork and descend steeply to a gravel track along the edge of salt marsh.

2. Continue ahead and follow the waymarked track around Salt House Farm. After crossing a cattle grid, look out for a waymark post to the right of the track. Turn right and climb a grassy bank to a stile into woods. Follow a narrow but clear woodland path steeply uphill.

3. Cross a stile at the top edge of the trees and another, immediately to the right. Turn left, along the edge of the field, then drop straight down the middle of a second field to a stone stile opposite a caravan park. Cross the A4066 and follow the grass verge to the right.

4. Turn left on to a minor road signed to Llansadurnen. At a lay-by, bear right to a stile into a field and follow the bottom edge to a stile at its end. Do not cross, but bear left towards a waymark post by a hedge corner. Follow the hedge to the right and join a grassy sunken track.

5. Go through a gate and continue down a stony track to a house. Keep ahead along the drive and down a tarmac lane to a junction. Turn right towards the edge of Laugharne, bearing left on to a smaller road by a triangle of grass. At a sharp right-hand bend, bear left on to a narrow, dead-end street ('Holloway Road').

6. Keep ahead on to a clear path, crossing two fields to a junction with Horsepool Lane. Turn right and then right again, along Laugharne's main street. Cross to the lych gate into St Martin's Church and climb to a kissing gate in the top left-hand corner of the churchyard (cross the footbridge on the right to visit Dylan Thomas's grave).

7. Turn left on to a lane. Climb to a junction and turn right, joining the descending farm track to Delacorse. Follow waymarks past the house and into a field. A clear path continues along the bottom edge of fields, just above the River Taf. Pass through a kissing gate and join a gravel path through woodland.

8. Emerge on a lane and follow it past the Dylan Thomas Boathouse and writing shed. Turn left at a junction and then left again. In front of Coach House, turn left into a narrow alley and descend to a track below Laugharne Castle. Bear right to return to the car park.

Where to eat and drink

Whether you're after a cup of tea or something stronger, there's plenty of choice to be had in Laugharne. For any Dylan Thomas fan, a pint in the poet's former local, Brown's Hotel, is surely essential. The pub has been tastefully modernised so as to retain its original character and offers bar food and a range of real Welsh ale.

What to see

Looking ahead from Salt House Farm you will be able to see Coygen Quarry. Before quarrying began here, there was an extensive cave system extending deep into an outcrop of carboniferous limestone. Stone tools discovered in the cave show that it was used by Neanderthal people between 60,000 and 40,000 years ago.

While you're there

A walk round the town is highly recommended. Laugharne Castle is a converted Tudor mansion badly damaged during the Civil War and contains a garden summer house used as a writing room by Dylan Thomas and Richard Hughes in the 1930s.

HIGH UP IN THE PRESELI HILLS

15

DISTANCE/TIME	5.5 miles (8.8km) / 2hrs 30min
ASCENT/GRADIENT	560ft (171m) / ▲ ▲ ▲
PATHS	Mainly clear paths across open moorland
LANDSCAPE	Rolling hills topped with rocky outcrops
SUGGESTED MAP	OS Explorer OL35 North Pembrokeshire
START/FINISH	Grid reference: SN165331
DOG FRIENDLINESS	Care needed near livestock
PARKING	Lay-by on lane beneath Foel Drygarn
PUBLIC TOILETS	None on route
NOTES	Difficult navigation in poor visibility

A circular walk around the most interesting sites of the Preseli Hills is almost impossible. The uplands form an isolated east-west ridge that would at best form one side of a circuit linked with a lengthy road section. Instead, this walk forms a contorted and narrow figure-of-eight that scales the most spectacular hill on the ridge, traces the line of the famous dolerite outcrops, or carns, and then makes an out-and-back sortie to an impressive stone circle.

The Pembrokeshire Coast National Park is best known for its stunning coastline. Britain's smallest national park is in no single place further than 10 miles (16km) from the sea. This furthest point was a deliberate extension of the boundaries to incorporate one of the most important historic sites in the United Kingdom, the Preseli Hills.

It was from Carn Menyn, one of the rocky tors that crown the marshy and often windswept hills, that the bluestones forming the inner circle of Stonehenge were taken. These bluestones, or spotted dolerite stones to give them their proper name, would have each weighed somewhere in the region of four tonnes and must have been transported over 200 miles (320km) in total. To this day, we cannot explain how or why.

The track that follows the ridge is an ancient road, perhaps dating back over 5,000 years. It's probable that it was a safe passage between the coast and the settlements inland at a time when wild predators such as bears and wolves roamed the valleys below. Gravestones line the track, most likely those of travellers or traders who were buried where they died, and other standing stones dot the hillsides.

West of Carn Menyn, beneath another impressive outcrop named Carn Bica, there's a stone circle known as Beddarthur. Small by comparison to Stonehenge or Avebury, its oval arrangement of 2ft–3ft (0.6m–1m) high stones is said to be yet another burial place of King Arthur; 'bedd' means grave in Welsh. There are certainly links between the legendary historical superhero and the area; it's suggested that the King and his knights chased Twrch Trywyth, the magical giant boar, across these hills before heading east.

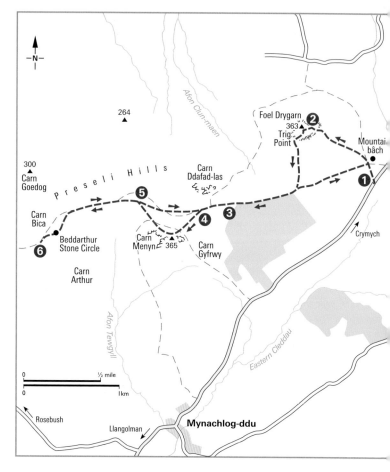

1. From the lay-by on the lane from Crymych, walk straight up a stony track opposite. When you reach three gates, keep going straight ahead for another 100yds (91m) or so, and then fork left on to a grassy track, which soon becomes clearer as it winds its way up the hillside. Follow this all the way to the rocky cairns and trig point on Foel Drygarn.

2. Bear left at the summit and locate a grassy track that drops steeply to the south. Cross the heather-clad plateau beneath, aiming for the left-hand corner of a wood. When you meet the main track, turn right to walk with the edge of the wood on your left.

3. Leaving the wood, the path climbs slightly to some rocky tors. As you pass the tor to the left of the track, the path forks and you follow the left-hand track to the nearest of the group of outcrops to your left.

4. This is Carn Gyfrwy. Continue on faint paths to the larger outcrops ahead, then curve right away from the stones and drop slightly to Carn Menyn, the lowest of the bunch, perched precariously on the edge of the escarpment. The path becomes clearer here and drops slightly into a marshy saddle that can be seen ahead.

5. In the saddle you'll meet the main track. Turn left and follow it steadily up towards Carn Bica, which is visible on the hillside ahead of you. Just before this, you'll cross the circle made by the stones of Beddarthur.

6. Turn around and retrace your steps back to the saddle. Climb slightly to pass the tor where you turned left to Carn Gyfrwy on your way out, ignoring the paths forking right to Carn Menyn, and stay on this main path to walk beside the wood once more, now on your right. At the end of this, continue straight on, following a fence-topped wall to your right, down to the gate. Turn right on to the lane and continue back to the lay-by.

Where to eat and drink

There's nothing on the route so it's best to head west to Rosebush where the community-run Tafarn Sinc does good food and welcomes children in the eating area before 9pm. There's also decent food to be found at the New Inn (Tafarn Newydd) on the main road on the other side of the village.

While you're there

Slate quarrying was once big business in the Preseli Hills and the remnants of this activity are still visible in places like Rosebush, to the west. If you'd like to see the kind of thing that can be crafted out of the smooth, flat stones, take a look at the Slate Workshop at Llangolman, where authentic Welsh slate is still put to good effect in a variety of craft items.

NEW QUAY AND CWMTYDU

16

DISTANCE/TIME	6.75 miles (10.9km) / 3hrs
ASCENT/GRADIENT	1,350ft (410m) / ▲▲▲
PATHS	Well-defined coastal paths and tracks; some lane walking
LANDSCAPE	Rugged cliffs, picturesque coves, secluded coastal valley
SUGGESTED MAP	OS Explorer 198 Cardigan & New Quay
START/FINISH	Grid reference: SN387598
DOG FRIENDLINESS	Can run free on coast path
PARKING	Large pay-and-display car park on the outskirts of New Quay
PUBLIC TOILETS	Seasonal toilets at start and just off the route in Cwmtydu; all-year facilities in New Quay itself

Many visitors to West Wales head straight for Pembrokeshire, bypassing the Ceredigion coastline a short distance to the north. They are missing a treat: at its best, the coastal walking in Ceredigion is the equal of anywhere in Wales. The spectacular stretch of coastline to the south of New Quay is a case in point. Here are dramatic cliffs and delightful hidden valleys, fabulous coastal vistas and picturesque coves. This part of Cardigan Bay is also one of the most important wildlife areas on the Welsh coast.

On the high cliffs west of New Quay you will pass a glass-fronted stone hut: the Cardigan Bay Lookout. This former coastguard hut is the perfect place to sit and shelter from the elements on a blustery day and watch the sea. If you are lucky, you may spot a porpoise or one of Cardigan Bay's semi-resident population of bottlenose dolphins. Over 300 of these majestic creatures are known to frequent the bay, with around 200 present in any year. Numbers increase throughout the summer, peaking in late September and October. Cardigan Bay's other resident marine mammal is the Atlantic grey seal. You may spot a seal on the rocks or swimming close to shore at any time of year, but the best time to see them is during August, when they haul themselves on to the rocky beaches below the cliffs to calve. The Ceredigion coast is known for its sea caves, which provide a safe and secluded area for the seals to give birth to their young.

It is worth watching the sky as well as the sea. Birds Rock, immediately below the lookout, is the most important seabird colony in Ceredigion and ranked among the top ten sites in Wales. Between March and July, hundreds of guillemots and razorbills nest precariously on the bare ledges, diving for fish in the waters below. In May, they are joined by kittiwakes, a gentle-looking, medium-sized gull that spends much of its time at sea outside the breeding season. Smaller species such as the chough and stonechat can be seen along the cliffs throughout the year.

On the return leg, the walk dips into Cwm Silio, a lovely coastal valley comprising a variety of grassland and broadleaved woodland habitats. In spring, the valley is awash with wild flowers and colourful butterflies. One of the rarest of the latter is the pearl-bordered fritillary, which flies between late April and the end of May. Other interesting insects you may spot include the forester moth, the Welsh chafer (a type of beetle), the giant lacewing and the enormous gold-ringed dragonfly.

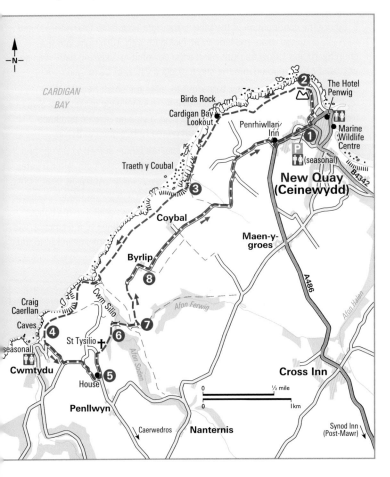

1. Turn right out of the car park to reach a right-hand bend. Bear left into Church Street and then immediately left again into Mason's Square. Follow the right-hand bend into Water Street and take the next road on the left (Lewis Terrace). Keep ahead to the end of a private road and join the signed coast path to Cwmtydu.

2. Climb steeply and continue along a clear clifftop path. The path divides to provide an alternative route away from an exposed cliff edge, rejoining near the Cardigan Bay Lookout. Past the lookout, continue along the right-hand edge of fields and drop steeply to a footbridge across a stream.

3. Keep following coast path signs until you reach a small bay at the mouth of a steep-sided valley (Cwm Silio). Bear right to cross a small river by a footbridge and climb steps to continue round the next headland. There is no one clear path for a while, but keep the sea to the right and you can't go too wrong.

4. At a fork above Cwmtydu, leave the coast path by continuing straight ahead. Shortly meet a lane and bear left up the hill. Continue along this lane until you reach a right-hand bend by a house.

5. Ignore the continuation of the lane to the right (signed to Caerwedros) and turn left on to the dead-end lane to St Tysilio Church. Turn right into the churchyard and follow its right-hand edge downhill to a kissing gate. Join an enclosed path dropping into the steep wooded valley of Cwm Silio.

6. At the bottom of the valley, turn right to cross the small river by a footbridge. Bear left, then immediately right, to join a wide gravel path away from the river. Cross another footbridge over a smaller stream and keep ahead to a waymark post. Take the path on the right signed to Byrlip.

7. At the next footpath junction, turn sharply left (again signed to Byrlip) and climb diagonally across the slope of the valley on a grassy path. After a gate, the path becomes enclosed and may be muddy in winter. At Byrlip, bear right between buildings and keep straight up the hill on to a gravel track.

8. The track levels off after a left-hand bend and runs parallel to the coast. Keep ahead on to a tarmac lane above Coybal and continue to a T-junction with the A486 by the Penrhiwllan Inn. Turn left and follow the road downhill to the car park on the outskirts of New Quay.

Where to eat and drink
There's a seasonal café around the halfway point in Cwmtydu, and plenty of choice at the end of the walk in New Quay, ranging from pubs and bars, fish and chip takeaways to ice cream parlours. For sea views, try the Hotel Penwig – it's a bit more pricey, but offers good food and has a light, airy bar overlooking Newquay Harbour.

What to see
The rocks that form the cliffs around Cwmtydu were laid down some 400 million years ago, during the Silurian era. Weaker points in the rock have buckled and crumpled, eroding into caves. These were used to hide smuggled brandy in the 18th century.

While you're there
After the walk, take a stroll down the hill into New Quay. There's a heritage centre and a marine wildlife centre, while a waymarked walk around the town explores Dylan Thomas's connections with the area.

RHOSSILI BAY

DISTANCE/TIME	4 miles (6.4km) / 1hr 45min
ASCENT/GRADIENT	590ft (180m) / ▲ ▲
PATHS	Easy-to-follow footpaths across grassy downs
LANDSCAPE	Rolling downland, rocky outcrops and views over gorgeous sandy beach
SUGGESTED MAP	OS Explorer 164 Gower
START/FINISH	Grid reference: SS416880
DOG FRIENDLINESS	Care needed near livestock
PARKING	Large car park at end of road in Rhossili
PUBLIC TOILETS	At start near National Trust shop

The Gower Peninsula comprises a 15-mile (24km) finger of land that points westwards from the urban sprawl of Swansea. Its southern coast is the more spectacular, boasting dune-backed beaches of surf-swept, clean, yellow sand and magnificent limestone cliffs, chiselled in places into deep gullies and knife-edge ridges. The northern coast forms the southern fringes of the marshy Loughor Estuary. It's nothing like as dramatic as the southern coast, but it's an important habitat for wading birds and other marine life. Between the two coastlines, the land rises into a series of whaleback ridges, or downs, covered with gorse, heather and bracken and littered with prehistoric stones and remains. Scattered around the windswept landscape are a number of impressive castles. In 1957, the peninsula was designated Britain's first Area of Outstanding Natural Beauty (AONB) or their new name National Landscapes.

Of all the Gower beaches, none are blessed with quite the untamed splendour of Rhossili Bay. It's sweeping expanse of golden sand runs for over 4 miles (6.4km) from the headland of the Worms Head to the stranded outcrop of Burry Holms, upon which sits a ruined monastic chapel. It owes much of its wild nature to the steep-sided down that presides over its relentless waves and provides a natural and impenetrable barrier to development. The down is a 633ft (193m) high, whaleback ridge that runs almost the full length of the beach. The path that traces the ridge is one the fairest places to walk in the whole of South Wales, especially in late summer when the heather tinges the hillsides pink. From The Beacon, at the southern end of the ridge, the views stretch a long way and it's often possible to see St Govan's Head in Pembrokeshire and even the North Devon coastline on a very clear day.

The string of tiny islets at the bay's southernmost tip are known as the Worms Head, the name deriving from the Old English, Orm, which means dragon or serpent. It is now a nature reserve, but can be reached at low tide by scrambling across the rocky causeway at the western tip of the promontory. It's essential that you check the tide timetables before making such a trip as it's easy to be cut off by the surprising tenacity of the rising tides.

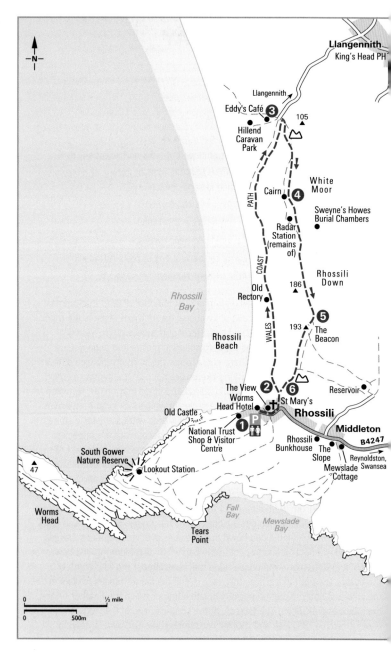

1. From the car park, head out on to the road and continue uphill as if you were walking back out of the village. You'll pass St Mary's Church on your left then, immediately after this, bear left down on a broad track to a gate at its end. Go through this and keep left to follow a grassy track that snakes along the steep hillside.

2. Follow this through the bracken, passing the Old Rectory on your left and eventually you'll reach a sunken section with a wall on your left, and a caravan park behind. Don't be tempted to break off right just yet; instead, keep going until you come to a gate by a road on the left.

3. Don't go through but turn sharp right and follow the grassy track steeply up on to the ridge. At the top of the steep section, where the path isn't always clear, it's easy to be drawn off to the right towards some obvious outcrops, but keep to the top track that literally follows the crest.

4. You'll pass some ancient cairns and drop slightly to pass a pair of megalithic cromlechs, or burial chambers. These are known as Sweyne's Howes and are over 4,000 years old. More obviously, you'll spot the remains of a World War II radar station to the right. Continue on a broad track up to the high point of The Beacon.

5. Keep straight ahead on a clear track that starts to drop easily then steepens to meet a dry-stone wall. Continue walking down the side of the wall and you'll eventually come to the gate you passed through on the way out.

6. Follow the lane out to the road, turn right and pass St Mary's Church on your right to return to the car park.

Where to eat and drink
One option is to walk 0.5 miles (800m) from Point 3 to Llangennith village, where the excellent, dog-friendly King's Head serves great food and real ale. Otherwise, there are a few places to get a hot drink and a snack in Rhossili, such as from The Lookout, offering tea, coffee, cake, sandwiches and ice cream, and the excellent The View, which serves breakfast and lunches during the day and restaurant food in the evenings. The Worms Head Hotel is the only pub in the village, but if you don't mind driving a few miles, the King Arthur Hotel at Reynoldston has a better atmosphere and serves better food. None of the Rhossili options are dog friendly.

What to see
More than one ship has fallen foul of the cruel storms that pound Rhossili and the wreckage of a few of these still pepper the beach. The most obvious is the Helvetica, now a crumbled timber skeleton protruding from the sands at low tide. She was washed up here in November 1887, but miraculously her five-man crew all survived.

While you're there
About 0.5 miles (800m) east of Reynoldston there's a footpath that leads to King Arthur's Stone, one of the finest standing cromlechs (burial chambers) in Wales, covered with an enormous capstone. The site is believed to be over 6,000 years old and is most striking when visited at sunrise or sunset.

PORT EYNON
TO RHOSSILI

DISTANCE/TIME	6.5 miles (10.4km) / 3hrs
ASCENT/GRADIENT	850ft (259m) / ▲ ▲
PATHS	Coast paths
LANDSCAPE	Limestone cliffs and sheltered bays
SUGGESTED MAP	OS Explorer 164 Gower
START	Grid reference: SS467851
FINISH	Grid reference: SS416881
DOG FRIENDLINESS	Care around livestock and on steep cliffs
PARKING	Large car park in Port Eynon
PUBLIC TOILETS	Near the start in Port Eynon and at Rhossili

The stretch of coast from Port Eynon along to Rhossili marks the far southwestern extent of the Gower peninsula and includes one of the most iconic sights in Wales: Worms Head. The sandy beach of Port Eynon Bay, though far from large, somehow manages to encompass two villages – Horton and Port Eynon, from where this walk sets off. While less undulating than some of the coastal paths around South Wales, there are still enough dips and climbs in the middle section of this route to get the heart pumping as you pass a brace of Iron Age forts and Paviland Cave, once erroneously believed to be the last resting place of the bones of the Red Lady of Paviland. Journey's end is at Rhossili, a tiny village popular with day-trippers, where refreshment awaits, along with a bus to take you back to Port Eynon at the end of the day.

In Victorian times, Port Eynon was a bustling place whose men worked in local quarries, fished for oyster or served as mariners. The place is a lot quieter now – the sandy beach now providing the main attraction. The 12th-century church of St Cattwg is also worth a gander before you set off. Though 'renovated' by the Victorians in their habitually intrusive manner, they didn't touch the Norman doorway and in the porch you can still see the stoup (for holding holy water), which is reputed to have been donated by a Spanish sea captain saved from drowning by local people.

A mile-long island spearing the Bristol Channel, Worms Head can be reached at low tide by crossing a rocky natural causeway. Forget any ideas you might have about the island looking like a worm, however. The name is a corruption of the Old English 'wyrm', meaning dragon. It was on the slopes below the fort on Worms Head that a young Dylan Thomas fell asleep, missed the tide and had to wait from dusk until midnight until the next one, fortified only by a bag of sandwiches and a book. He later recalled being terrified by the experience and he left as soon as the tide went out sufficiently for him to creep back over to the mainland. However, he clearly came to terms with the encounter because the Worms Head featured in Thomas' short story *Who Do You Wish Was With Us?*

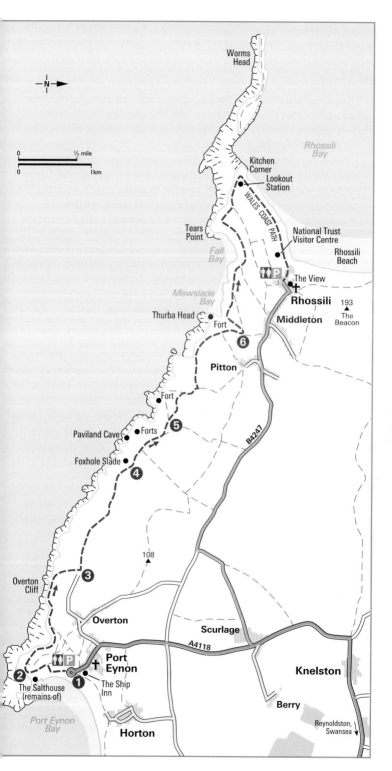

Worms
Head

*Rhossili
Bay*

Kitchen
Corner
Lookout
Station

WALES COAST PATH

Tears
Point

National Trust
Visitor Centre

Rhossili
Beach

*Fall
Bay*

The View

*Mewslade
Bay*

Rhossili

193
▲
The
Beacon

Thurba Head

Fort

❻

Middleton

Pitton

Fort

❺

Paviland Cave

Forts

B4247

Foxhole Slade

❹

Overton
Cliff

108
▲

❸

Overton

Scurlage

A4118

Knelston

🚻 P

❷

**Port
Eynon**

The Salthouse
(remains of)

❶

The Ship
Inn

Berry

Reynoldston,
Swansea ↓

*Port Eynon
Bay*

Horton

—N→

0   ½ mile
0   1 km

1. At low tide, walk on to the beach following 'coast path' waymarkers to the obvious ruins of the Salthouse on the point, where an information board gives plenty of interesting history on the area. If the tide's high, follow a good track past the car park and through a gate to the Youth Hostel, which you keep to your left to continue on a caravan park drive to the ruins down on your left. From here, follow the sandy track along the coast until, in the centre of the rocky bay to your left, the path splits. Take the right-hand fork and climb up steeply taking the left fork when the path splits again past a quarry on your right to the monument on the hilltop.

2. Follow the cliff tops until the path drops down to a gate. Cross this and walk behind the rocky beach. Ignore the path off to the right half-way across the beach and when the path forks, keep left to another gate marked Overton Cliffs. Keep ahead to follow the path as it squeezes between impressive limestone cliffs and steep scree. You'll hurdle a wonderful rocky terrace and drop beneath more formidable crags, many of which make for excellent rock climbing. The path sneaks between more rocky outcrops before heading down to a wall. Go through the gate, turn right and follow the path steeply upwards to meet a good path.

3. Turn left on to this and follow the wall. Continue to follow the coast path, until you reach the deeply cloven gorge of Foxhole Slade.

4. Keep ahead in the dip through a gate and climb steeply back up. This area is owned by the National Trust and to your left, but almost impossible to reach, is Paviland Cave. Continue along the wall and through another gate. After 100yds (91m), next to a wooden gate on the right, fork left and continue until you join the wall again and drop to a gate. Cross this and bear left to head back out on to the cliff top.

5. Here you'll find the obvious earthworks of an Iron Age fort. A wall splits the ramparts; cross this through a gate and follow the coast around to a fence, which you then follow to the head of a huge hollow with no name on the OS map. Go behind this, bearing slightly right at the crossroads of paths by a stile (which you don't cross) and continue along the line of the wall, which initially hugs the coast before heading back inland a little as it approaches Mew Slade. There are more ancient earthworks on Thurba Head, to your left. As the wall turns sharp right, keep straight ahead to a steep path that drops down some-what awkwardly into Mew Slade.

6. From the bottom of the dip, vertigo sufferers would be best advised to continue along the coast path to avoid an extremely narrow path above a precipitous drop. Everyone else should turn left after the gate to follow a grassy path coastwards to the small cove, hidden behind rocky outcrops and covered almost completely by the sea at high tide. A narrow path heads west from the beach and contours around the steep hillside to rejoin the main coast path (and any vertigo sufferers) in an area of outstanding limestone scenery. Bear left on to the path here and follow it around to another dip. Keep high to round the head of the valley and then drop down, towards Tears Point. Head back up the grassy down towards the cliff tops, where you veer around to the right to follow them along. Continue around the coast passing above Worms Head and then swinging north at Kitchen Corner to rejoin the main, well-surfaced track as you approach Rhossili village. Continue past the information centre and the main car park to the bus stop, on the left just before the church.

Where to eat and drink

Port Eynon has only one pub, The Ship Inn. There are a few snack options around the beach if you're after really casual or the Smuggler's Beach Bar & Kitchen if you want something a little more civilised. Alternatively eat in Rhossili or travel to Reynoldston.

What to see

The limestone cliffs of the Gower coast are justly popular with rock climbers. Along this section are a number of well-known routes that span from easy, beginner's climbs to high-grade test pieces. If the weather's fine, you're almost bound to spot some activity as you walk.

While you're there

The National Trust information centre at Rhossili, in a converted coastguard building, contains a large shop and displays about their work on the Gower. It also has tide times that will be useful if you intend crossing on to the Worms Head.

Paviland Cave is where a headless body was once discovered. It was originally thought to be female and nicknamed the Red Lady of Paviland, as the bones were stained red. Modern tests show that the skeleton was actually male and carbon dating puts it at some 24,000 years old. Exploration of the area above the cave, which isn't safe to reach, revealed the ditches and ramparts of an ancient settlement.

19

WOODLAND
AT OXWICH POINT

DISTANCE/TIME	4.5 miles (7.2km) / 2hrs
ASCENT/GRADIENT	480ft (146m) / ▲ ▲
PATHS	Clear paths through woodland, along coast and across farmland, quiet lane
LANDSCAPE	Mixed woodland and rugged coastline
SUGGESTED MAP	OS Explorer 164 Gower
START/FINISH	Grid reference: SS500864
DOG FRIENDLINESS	Can mostly run free but watch steep cliffs and livestock
PARKING	Oxwich Bay
PUBLIC TOILETS	Opposite Oxwich Bay Hotel near start

The Gower has less obvious headlands than nearby Pembrokeshire, so interesting circular walks are harder to come by. This one stands out for a couple of reasons. Firstly, it can be combined with a visit to Oxwich National Nature Reserve, a treasure trove of marshland and sand dunes in a wonderful beachside location. Secondly, the wonderful coastal scenery includes the beautiful and usually deserted beach known as The Sands. And finally, being relatively short, it allows plenty of time for exploring both the atmospheric St Illtyd's Church and the majestic ruins of Oxwich Castle.

Once a busy port that paid its way by shipping limestone from quarries on the rugged headland, Oxwich is now one of the prettiest and most unspoilt Gower villages, due in no small part to its distance from the main roads. The name is derived from Axwick, Norse for water creek. For maximum enjoyment, it's best visited away from the main holiday seasons.

St Illtyd's Church, founded in the 6th century AD and tucked away in a leafy clearing above the beach, is particularly significant for its stone font, which is said to have been donated by St Illtyd himself. The grounds are tranquil with an atmosphere that comes in stark contrast to the summertime noise of the beach below. Behind the building is the grave of an unknown soldier who was washed up on the beach during World War II. It's certainly a spooky spot and the graveyard is purported to be haunted by a strange half-man-half-horse creature. St Illtyd (or St Illtud) was a Welsh-born monk who founded the nearby abbey of Llanilltud Fawr (Llantwit Major). He is perhaps most famous for his fights against famine, which included sailing grain ships to Brittany. He died in Brittany in AD 505.

Really a 16th-century mansion house built by Sir Rhys Mansel on the site of the 14th-century castle, Oxwich Castle occupies an airy setting above the bay. Sir Rhys, in common with many locals, wasn't above plundering the cargo of ships that came to grief in the bay and was quick to take advantage of a French wreck in late December 1557. The salvage rights, however, belonged to a Sir George Herbert of Swansea, who quickly paid Mansel a visit to reclaim his goods. A fight broke out and Sir Rhys's sister Anne was injured by a stone thrown by Herbert's servant. She later died from her injuries. There followed a feud which continued for many years until eventually the Mansel family moved to Margam, east of Swansea. Part of the mansion was leased to local farmers, but most of the fine building fell into disrepair.

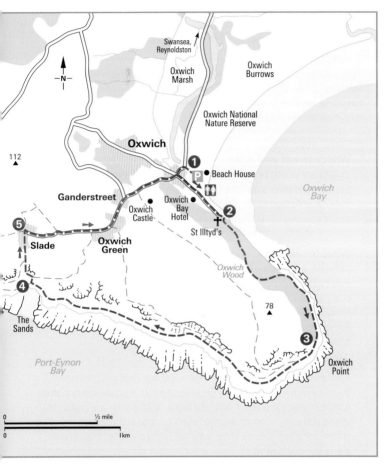

1. Walk back out of the car park and turn left to a crossroads. Turn left here (waymarked 'Eglwys') and pass the Oxwich Bay Hotel, on your right. This lane leads into the woods and up to St Illtyd's Church, where a gate marks the end of the road and the start of a path leading out on to Oxwich Point.

2. Join the path that runs beneath the church, and follow it for a few paces before going up wooden steps that climb steeply into the wood. Just before the top of the steps, turn left to go through the wood, dropping back down a veritable glut of steps and around the headland until it comes out into the open above Oxwich Point.

3. The path drops through gorse and bracken to become a grassy coast path that runs easily above a rocky beach. Keep the sea on your left and ignore any tracks that run off to the right. After approximately 1 mile (1.6km), you'll pass a

distinct valley that drops in from your right. Continue past this and you'll be funnelled into a narrow, fenced section with a field to your right. Go through a couple of gates, and you'll eventually reach a path diversion that points you right, away from the beach.

4. Follow this to a kissing gate and a broad farm track, where you turn left. Continue up and around to the right until you come to a galvanised kissing gate. Go through this and keep right to head up a lane past some houses to a crossroads with a lane on your left marked Western Slade Farm.

5. Turn right here and follow the road along to a fork where you keep right. Pass through the hamlets of Oxwich Green and Ganderstreet. Drop down to the entrance of Oxwich Castle on the right. After looking at or exploring the castle, turn right, back on to the lane, and head down into Oxwich village. Keep straight ahead to the car park.

Where to eat and drink
Snacks are available in Oxwich – try the Beach House or the General Stores – and there's also the Oxwich Bay Hotel, which you pass on the walk, serving food all day from bar snacks to daily specials (children's meals also available). But, for the best food and atmosphere in this part of the Gower, it's worth heading to the King Arthur Hotel in Reynoldston.

What to see
Spring is a great time to wander the woods of Oxwich Point, where many interesting flowers can be seen vying for space before the deciduous canopy develops, cutting out the light supply. Perhaps the most prolific is ramsons, or wild garlic as it's also known. It isn't actually related to garlic, but when the woodland floor is completely carpeted by the stunning white flowers, the smell resembles it.

While you're there
A windswept pot-pourri of dunes, saltwater marshes and freshwater pools, Oxwich National Nature Reserve offers an unusual and important habitat to many species of flora and fauna. Wild orchids are prolific in spring and early summer and the reserve is also an important breeding ground for a few species of butterfly, including the small blue, brown argus and marbled white. There are a number of trails to explore that cross the marshes.

20

PENNARD, ILSTON AND BISHOPSTON VALLEY

DISTANCE/TIME	9.25 miles (14.9km) / 3hrs 45min
ASCENT/GRADIENT	1,250ft (380m) / ▲ ▲
PATHS	Rough, stony path in Bishopston Valley; slippery in wet weather (1 stile)
LANDSCAPE	Coastal common, dunes, wooded valleys, fabulous sea views
SUGGESTED MAP	OS Explorer 164 Gower
START/FINISH	Grid reference: SS553873
DOG FRIENDLINESS	Livestock on coastal cliffs, but can run free in woods
PARKING	Pay-and-display car park in Southgate
PUBLIC TOILETS	Opposite car park at start of walk

The Gower Peninsula is a place of stunning and astonishingly varied natural beauty. Here are hidden coves and glorious sandy beaches, high cliffs and windswept downs, dunes, marshland, wooded valleys and picturesque villages. Almost every path opens up a new and rewarding perspective, but there is no walk on Gower that captures this amazing variety better than this one.

To the west of Pennard, the view over Three Cliffs Bay will literally take your breath away. High above this fabulous beach (regularly voted among the best in Britain) perch the ruins of Pennard Castle. This dramatic ruin was probably built in the late 13th century to replace an earlier ringwork defence. It seemed like an ideal location, but the castle's Norman lords could not have foreseen the problem of encroaching sand. Advancing sand dunes destroyed the fertility of the surrounding land and by the 15th century, the castle had been abandoned.

In 1649, St Illtyd's Church, Ilston, became home to the first Baptist congregation in Wales. Its new rector, John Myles, was a supporter of Cromwell and went on to found a number of Baptist churches in South Wales during the Civil War. After the Restoration, Myles was ejected from his Ilston living and forced to hold his Baptist meetings at the small pre-Reformation chapel lower down Ilston Cwm. Persecution continued and the congregation eventually dispersed in 1664. Taking with him the Ilston Book – a register of all 261 members of Ilston's Baptist congregation – Myles emigrated to America and founded a town in Massachusetts called Swansea, where he served as the town's first minister and then schoolmaster until his death in 1684. Now held by Brown University of Providence, Rhode Island, the Ilston Book is no longer available for public viewing but a transcript of its contents is held by the National Library of Wales in Aberystwyth.

Now densely wooded, the Bishopston Valley was at one time divided into fields by dry-stone walls; even today there are areas of meadowland in the forest grazed by cattle. The valley's most interesting feature is its stream, which disappears underground near Bishopston Church, where it meets the pervious limestone rocks underlying the valley. It reappears after reaching more impervious rocks further down the valley.

At Guzzle Hole, the underground stream can be seen and heard from the entrance to a shallow limestone cave (the name refers to the 'guzzling' sound made by the running water). Limestone was a valuable commodity in the 19th century, and over 200 hundred men were employed at a coastal quarry in Pwlldu Bay.

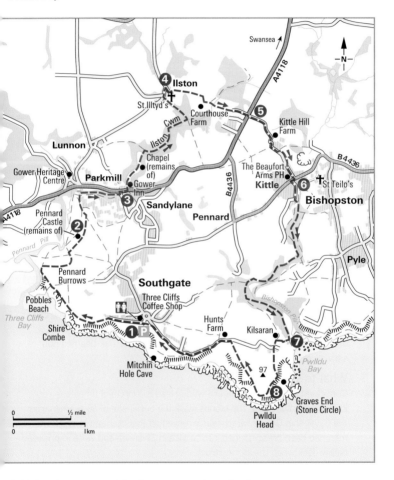

1. Facing the sea, turn right along a tarmac lane. Continue on to a grassy clifftop, which curves right above Pobbles Beach ('Wales Coast Path'). Follow a grassy/sandy path into a valley. Turn left, then right, and climb steeply. Join a boardwalk above Three Cliffs Bay and follow the high ground above Pennard Pill to Pennard Castle.

2. Keep ahead to reach an enclosed path to the left of chalets. Descend steeply through woodland to a junction of paths and turn right. Follow a stream to a junction with a lane and cross to a track opposite. Drop to a footbridge and turn right along the A4118 (no pavement).

3. Just before the Gower Inn, take a path on the left ('Ilston'). Walk up Ilston Cwm to the remains of a chapel, crossing two footbridges. Continue up the valley, crossing four further bridges to reach a waymarked fork. Turn left and follow the main stream to St Illtyd's Church, Ilston. Walk through the graveyard and turn right.

4. At a small green, turn right up a track. With a house ahead, turn sharp left and join an enclosed path. At a grassy track, turn right towards Courthouse Farm and then sharp left, along the stony access track. Follow this down to a stream and then up to the A4118.

5. Keep straight across on to a road signed to Kittle. At Kittle Hill Farm, follow the lane round a series of bends, then go through a kissing gate on the left. The path runs parallel to the road, rejoining it in Kittle. Continue to a T-junction by the Beaufort Arms.

6. Turn right and cross to a footpath sign for the Bishopston Valley. Follow a track to a house and continue on a path to the left. Shortly fork left and descend past Gulver Pit to the dry, rocky bed of Bishopston Pill. Turn right and follow the main path down the valley to Pwlldu Bay.

7. Turn right on to a steep, stony track climbing out of the bay ('Wales Coast Path'). Join an access track by Kilsaran house and climb to the left. At a right-hand bend, keep ahead on to a path signed to Pwlldu Head.

8. At the headland, drop steeply towards the sea. Bear right at a waymark post and climb to the top of cliffs. The path bears right again, crossing grassy clifftops to reach an unfenced lane near Hunts Farm. Turn left and follow the grassy common to the left of the lane back to Southgate.

Where to eat and drink
The Three Cliffs Coffee Shop in Southgate is justifiably popular with locals and visitors alike. If you like wholesome homemade food, you can't go wrong here. During the walk, you may want to stop for something stronger. The Beaufort Arms in Kittle is a traditional, oak-beamed pub serving excellent food and drink.

What to see
Concealed in the bracken near Pwlldu Head is a circle of limestone rocks known as Graves End. The stones mark the burial site of 68 seamen from the naval ship Caesar, which was wrecked off Pwlldu Head in 1760. The men had been press-ganged into service in Swansea and were imprisoned below deck when the storm struck.

While you're there
The Gower Heritage Centre in Parkmill is a crafts and rural life museum based around a renovated 12th-century corn and saw mill. The mill was powered by water from the stream flowing through Parc Cwm. The centre also has tea rooms and a range of local artisan shops.

CARREG CENNEN CASTLE

DISTANCE/TIME	4 miles (6.4km) / 2hrs
ASCENT/GRADIENT	590ft (180m) / ▲ ▲
PATHS	Good paths and tracks, many stiles
LANDSCAPE	Rolling pastures and deciduous woodland, short stretches of riverside
SUGGESTED MAP	OS Explorer 186 Llandeilo & Brechfa Forest; OS Explorer Llanelli & Ammanford; OS Explorer OL12 Brecon Beacons National Park
START/FINISH	Grid reference: SN666193
DOG FRIENDLINESS	Not welcome in castle grounds, most stiles not dog friendly, care needed near livestock
PARKING	Car park beneath castle
PUBLIC TOILETS	At start of the walk

Carreg Cennen is one of the most dramatically positioned castles in the whole of the principality. It occupies an airy perch atop precipitous limestone cliffs and commands fine views in all directions. Throughout this walk – which is helpfully marked all the way round by signposts bearing a red castle symbol – you're treated to many fleeting glimpses of the towering spectacle and then at the end you can actually explore the ruins themselves. Unusually for a Welsh castle, Carreg Cennen was built by the Welsh rather than the Normans. The first stronghold was constructed in the late 12th century, although legend tells of a fortress here during the reign of King Arthur, controlled by Urien Rheged and his son Owain. A Roman coin found on the site suggests an even earlier settlement. Just for good measure, there is meant to be a warrior asleep beneath the castle. This knight – who is possibly even King Arthur (if you're going to invent a myth you may as well aim high) – will apparently arise to save Wales in the nation's hour of greatest need.

Carreg Cennen changed hands several times before it was eventually seized by Edward I in 1277. A hundred or so years later, it was taken down and a new fortress built in its place by John Giffard. However, the fortunes of the castle remained the same – changing hands at a brisk rate, with owners including John of Gaunt and Henry of Bolingbroke, who went on to become King Henry IV. It also had time to fit in a siege around 1403 during the uprising staged by Owain Glyndŵr, when it took quite a beating.

During the Wars of the Roses, in the 15th century, the castle's owners sided with the Lancastrians. This proved an unfortunate decision and, after the eventual Yorkist victory in 1461, the castle was demolished brick by brick, stone by stone, to its current condition, apparently on the grounds that it had become a den for local bandits, miscreants and ne'er-do-wells and was a threat to the new order. Labour was certainly cheap in those days – 500 local men were paid £28 between them to complete the task.

Perhaps the most thrilling feature of the castle nowadays is a largely natural one. It's a limestone cave that can be reached down a set of steps close to the postern gate. The passageway has been lined with stone and the ceiling of the cave is vaulted with a dovecote built into a wall. Do remember to take along a torch if you want to explore the cave.

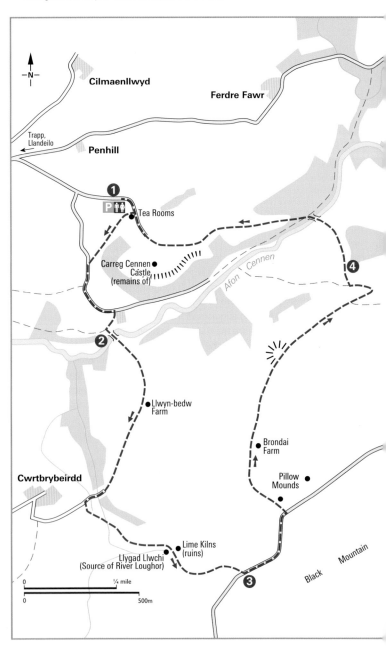

1. From the car park, head out of the gate at the top and proceed towards the castle. As you reach the part-white building on the right, turn right through a gate on to a footpath. Follow this diagonally leftwards, down to join the fence on the left-hand side of the field and down to a kissing gate that leads on to a road. Turn left and pass a footpath on your right to head around a left-hand bend. Before you reach the house on the right, turn right through a gate and walk down the centre of the field to a stile. Cross this to drop steeply down to another stile and across the field to a footbridge over the River Cennen.

2. Cross the bridge and climb steeply up towards the left-hand hedge where you cross an iron stile. Continue upwards, along the fence, to the top of the field where you bear right to follow it around, beneath Llwyn-bedw farm. This leads to an opening where you join an obvious farm track and bear right. Follow this across a cattle grid and over a shallow ford to another cattle grid. Climb up a short hill and, at the top, turn left over a stile. Follow the edge of the field and climb a stile. Cross the small stream and bear right up a stony track to a stile. Cross this, then the adjacent stile by the caving notice, to follow a narrow path down to the source of the River Loughor. This is an enchanted spot with the infant river gushing to freedom from the cave that imprisoned it for the formative stages of its life. Return to the two stiles and turn right, back on to the footpath, to continue past a ruined lime kiln on the left. Follow the track up and around to the left where it peters out into open pasture. Continue straight ahead between two huge dips in the ground to a stile, then bear half right, keeping a fenced-off shake hole to the left, to a stile and a narrow road.

3. Turn left and follow the road up over a cattle grid and around a left-hand bend. As the road swings right, turn left on to a clear farm track. Continue to where the drive bears right to the house and keep straight ahead, over a stile and alongside a grove of ash trees for 200yds (182m) to a gate. Turn right and follow the fenced path up the hillside. The views of the castle from here are among the best on the walk. Continue through a gate and then a stile and along a sunken path to join a stony track on a hairpin bend. Keep ahead (downhill) to another hairpin bend and round this then turn right, over a stile, to drop to a stream.

4. Bear left on the bank and cross a stile, a footbridge and another stile. This leads to a larger footbridge over the River Cennen. Turn right, then left on to a waymarked path that climbs up through oak trees towards the castle. From the entrance, follow the tarmac track down to the car park.

Where to eat and drink
The tea rooms by the car park is the only place for refreshment on the walk, or for more choice, visit Llandelio, which is 5 miles (8km) away.

What to see
As you turn from the road into the farm drive at the far end of the walk, the huge banks of earth and rock on the righthand side are referred to on the map as Pillow Mounds. These are thought to be the remains of a Bronze Age burial site, around 3000 BC, although another line of thought suggests that they could be nothing more sinister than commercially farmed rabbit warrens, a common practice in Victorian times.

22 THE ESCARPMENTS OF THE CARMARTHEN FAN

DISTANCE/TIME	7.5 miles (12.1km) / 4hrs 30min
ASCENT/GRADIENT	2,000ft (610m) / ▲ ▲ ▲
PATHS	Faint paths, trackless sections over open moorland
LANDSCAPE	Imposing mountains, hidden lakes, wild and remote moorland
SUGGESTED MAP	OS Explorer OL12 Brecon Beacons National Park
START/FINISH	Grid reference: SN798238
DOG FRIENDLINESS	Care needed near livestock and steep drops
PARKING	At end of small unclassified road, southeast of Llanddeusant
PUBLIC TOILETS	None on route
NOTES	Best avoided in poor visibility

The view eastwards from the flanks of Bannau Sir Gaer across Llyn y Fan Fach to the steepest section of the Carmarthen Fan is breathtaking. There's something special about the broody black waters, their shimmering surface reflecting skywards a rippled mirror image of the shattered crags of the escarpment. Ravens, buzzards and red kites ride high on the updraughts and the picture becomes all the more sinister for the addition of a little light cloud, drifting in and out of the summits.

You won't be the first to become bewitched by this lavish scene. The lake was visited regularly long ago by a local shepherd boy known as Rhiwallon. He encountered a mystical lady, as beautiful as the reflection in the lake that she'd risen from. Her wisdom matched her beauty and she possessed the ability to make healing potions from herbs and flowers. Rhiwallon was captivated, so much so that he proposed marriage and she agreed, but only on the condition that he should never strike her with iron. Rhiwallon and his wife had a son before the inevitable happened, perhaps by accident, and the lady returned to the dark waters, taking with her all of their worldly goods, including the animals they tended. Fortunately, before she left, she had passed on all of her medicinal skills to her son, who went on to become a local healer. Far fetched? Maybe, but it's interesting to note that much later on, the area did actually become renowned for its healers and there followed a long line of successful practitioners known as the Physicians of Myddfai (a village north of the lake).

From the narrow summit of Fan Foel, your grapple with gravity is rewarded by huge views across the bleak uplands of the Black Mountain (singular), not to be confused with the Black Mountains (plural) which are some 30 miles (48km) east of here and visible on a clear day. This is the westernmost mountain range of the National Park and, without doubt, the wildest and most remote. The majority of the land is made up of barren, windswept moorland that possesses an austere beauty with few equals.

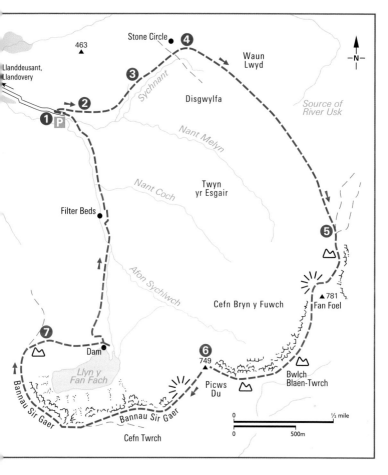

1. From the car park at the end of the unclassified road, head back towards Llanddeusant and after about 100yds (91m), turn sharp right, almost doubling back on yourself, to continue on a faint track that contours eastwards around the hillside. Follow this track as it then veers northeast into the small valley carved out over the centuries by the Sychnant brook.

2. The track becomes clearer, briefly. However, it is very easy to be seduced into surging up to the east here along the much more obvious valley of Nant Melyn. It's very important not to be fooled but to keep to the left bank of the smaller Sychnant, which turns to the northeast.

3. The track is faint but the going reasonably easy as you continue up the valley, crossing a small tributary and following the bank above the Sychnant. Numerous paths and sheep tracks cross your way, but continue unhindered upwards, aiming for the shallow saddle on the blunt ridge above. The stream eventually swings to the right and peters out. At this stage, bear right and head along the ridge.

4. You're now aiming for the steep and obvious spur of Fan Foel, which lies southeast of you, approximately 1.5 miles (2.4km) away. Follow whatever tracks you can find over Waun Lwyd and, as the ridge starts to narrow, keep to the crest where you'll meet a path coming up from the northeast.

5. Climb steeply up the narrow path on to the escarpment and keep right to follow the escarpment along. The path becomes clearer as it drops steeply into Bwlch Blaen-Twrch. From here, climb up on to Bannau Sir Gaer and continue to the summit cairn.

6. Stay with the main footpath and follow the edge of the escarpment above the precipitous cliffs into a small saddle or col and up again above Llyn y Fan Fach. Continue around the lake, with the steep drop to your right and you'll see a good path dropping down a grassy spur to the outflow of the lake.

7. Follow this obvious footpath and then, when you reach the dam, pick up the well-surfaced track that heads back downhill. This will lead you to the right of the filter beds and back to the car park.

Where to eat and drink

There is nowhere on the route to eat or drink however the local centres of Llandovery, Llangadog and Trecastle have pubs, cafés and restaurants where you can grab a bite to eat.

What to see

To the south of the escarpment, the old red sandstone that acts as a spine for most of the high ground in the Bannau Brycheiniog (Brecon Beacons), slips beneath a layer of much younger limestone. The distinctive light-coloured outcrops can easily be seen from this walk, especially looking southeast from the summit of Bannau Sir Gaer. Look closer for the potholes and caves that typify this environment – the suggested Ordnance Survey map for this area shows that it is pockmarked all the way to the Tawe Valley.

While you're there

The Dan-yr-Ogof Showcaves, on the A4067 near Glyntawe, are approximately 10 miles (16km) from the start of the walk. Claiming to be the largest cave system in Europe, the huge caverns are certainly spectacular. There are no guided tours, you simply walk yourself around, following a clear path between the stalactites and stalagmites, while listening to a recorded commentary. Other attractions on the site include a dinosaur park, Iron Age farm, a museum, shire horse centre and a covered children's play area. It's open daily between April to October.

DRYGARN FAWR

DISTANCE/TIME	9.5 miles (15.3km) / 6hrs
ASCENT/GRADIENT	2,000ft (610m) / ▲ ▲
PATHS	Riverside path, faint or non-existent paths over moorland, some good tracks, some awkward stream crossings
LANDSCAPE	Stunning valley, remote moorland, some forestry
SUGGESTED MAP	OS Explorer 200 Llandrindod Wells & Elan Valley
START/FINISH	Grid reference: SN860530
DOG FRIENDLINESS	Care needed near livestock
PARKING	Car park northeast of Abergwesyn
PUBLIC TOILETS	At start of the walk
NOTES	Difficult navigation in poor visibility

This is the toughest walk in the whole book, but more by the nature of the terrain than the amount of ascent. The rewards, for those who are prepared to navigate their way carefully over one short stretch of trackless moorland, are rich beyond description, for this is a foray into the wilder side of Wales – a place that sees few footprints. For less experienced walkers, this is definitely one to tackle only after you've cut your teeth on the high ground of Bannau Brycheiniog (Brecon Beacons), and then only in good visibility. Alternatively, if you're unsure about the navigation, or if you are in any doubt about the visibility, follow the outward leg on to Drygarn Fawr and return by retracing your steps.

The remote nature of the landscape links this area, more than any other, with one of Britain's most beautiful birds, the red kite. It was the scene of this most majestic raptor's final stand. Free of persecution, pesticides and disturbance, a mere handful defiantly resisted extinction by scavenging these moors and nesting in the abundance of trees that line the valleys. Their decline was thankfully halted by a number of conservation groups who, working closely with local landowners, started a release programme of birds imported from Scandinavia and Spain. Successful breeding in both England and Scotland began in 1992 and since then the population has increased so significantly they are almost common here today.

The birds are easily distinguished from the more common buzzard, which can also be seen in this area, as they are much slimmer in build with narrower, more angular wings and a distinct fork in the longer tail. The plumage is a mixture of russet red and chestnut brown with white wing patches and a silver head. Their flight is more agile and a close view will show the tail constantly twisting as if trimming a sail.

There are a handful of designated red kite feeding stations in the area, mostly operating in winter, so if you want to get closer to these beautiful birds, then search for times online.

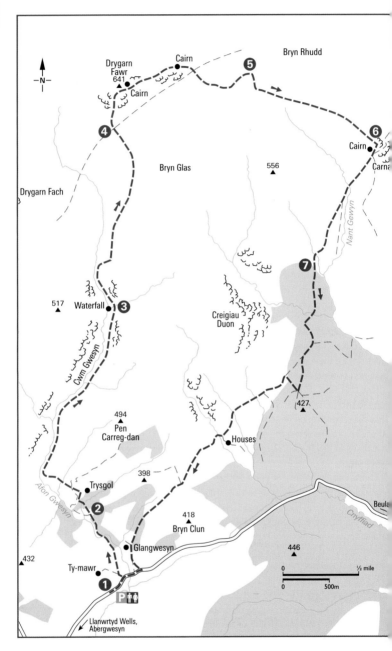

1. Turn right on to the road and walk towards the bridge, just before which a stony track heads up left. Take this and after 100yds (91m) turn right, through a gate. Follow the track across fields and down to the Afon Gwesyn, which you ford. Continue to a gate and up towards a wood where the track splits. Choose the top option and then, as this bends around to the left and heads downhill 20yds (18m) later, fork right, to traverse the clearing to a gap in the wood.

2. Follow the path down to a ford. Climb on to open ground and bear right to climb to a farm track by some buildings. Turn left on to this and follow it through a gate, where you fork left to walk beneath some crags. Ignore another fork to the left and continue to open ground. Follow the east side of the valley for over 1.5 miles (2.4km) to a waterfall.

3. Pass this on the right, then continue until the path almost disappears. Follow the line of the stream until you reach a distinctive small ridge coming in from the right. Take this uphill for 150yds (135m) and then bear left on to a narrow path, which leads you around a number of boggy patches until the cairned summit of Drygarn Fawr becomes visible. The path is often very indistinct. If you become unsure, aim for the crags and use a compass.

4. Climb the grassy slope to the trig point, then follow the ridge east past both cairns. A close scan of the hillsides to the east-southeast should reveal two grassy tops, 1.5 miles (2.4km) away, one with a large cairn on top – this is Carnau, your next objective. A clear grassy track descends east from the cairn. Follow this until it levels completely and rounds a left-hand bend, where you'll make out a faint path forking right. This is the start of the careful navigation and if you're in any doubt about visibility, or your ability to navigate, you'll be better off turning around and retracing your tracks.

5. Follow the track, which passes to the left of a solitary boundary marker. Turn sharp right here (south), away from the path, and cross wet ground to climb slightly on to a very broad rounded ridge. You'll make out the head of a small valley ahead and, as you drop into this, bear slightly left to follow the high ground with the valley to your right. Continue on sheep tracks to cross a couple of hollows, until you reach a grassy hilltop on your left. From here, you should be able to see the cairn ahead. Take the clear path that leads to it. Alternatively, keep as straight a line as you can from the cairn, with your eyes fixed on Carnau and your compass to the fore.

6. From Carnau, you'll see the start of a clear gorge away to the southwest. Walk towards this, on a visible path, and you'll pick up a good track as you cross the river. Continue downstream on the far bank and then stay with the path as it bears away right and crosses open hillsides. Take a right when the path forks in order to drop into the bottom of the valley, where you need to ford the stream to go through a gate.

7. Climb on a good track that eventually drops to cross another stream via a footbridge and then continue up to a five-way junction. Turn sharp right here, go through a gate and then another on the left. Drop down through the field past a sheepfold and through three gates and on to an enclosed track and follow this to a junction above some houses on your left. Keep right, going onto a grassy path, cross a stream and then take the track across a field to a path junction. By a cluster of gates, go through three to keep straight ahead and descend through the yard of Glangwesyn to the road. Turn right on to the road to return to your car.

Where to eat and drink

The Neuadd Arms Hotel in Llanwrtyd Wells is a haven for walkers has a choice of two bars, both serving fine ales and good home cooked meals.

AROUND
THE TEIFI POOLS

DISTANCE/TIME	6.25 miles (10km) / 3hrs
ASCENT/GRADIENT	1,000ft (300m) / ▲ ▲
PATHS	Moorland bridleways and surfaced tracks, boggy in places (2 stiles)
LANDSCAPE	Mountain lakes, open moorland, upland river valleys
SUGGESTED MAP	OS Explorer 187 Llandovery and OS Explorer 213 Aberystwyth & Cwm Rheidol
START/FINISH	Grid reference: SN769655
DOG FRIENDLINESS	Mostly open country, though dogs will need to be kept on a lead near sheep
PARKING	Small lay-by 1.7 miles (2.75km) east of Strata Florida abbey, just west of Tyncwm farm
PUBLIC TOILETS	None on route

The Teifi Pools is the collective name for a group of small lakes (some of which have been enlarged by dams) high up in the hills to the east of Pontrhydfendigaid. The lakes, which are popular with fishermen and possess a stark, austere beauty, lie some 1,500ft (450m) above sea level in an area of wild, open moorland often referred to as Wales' 'green desert'. The largest of the lakes, Llyn Teifi, is traditionally considered to be the source of the Afon Teifi, at 76 miles (122km), the longest Welsh river wholly within Wales.

Driving up the Teifi Valley from Pontrhydfendigaid (known colloquially as 'Bont'), you will pass the former Cistercian abbey of Strata Florida. Founded in 1164 under the patronage of the Lord Rhys (1132–1164), a native Welsh prince of Deheubarth, the abbey developed into one of the great buildings of medieval Wales. Under Rhys and his successors, it also acted as a focus for resistance to Anglo-Norman occupation.

The abbey's significance derived from the loss of St Davids to the Normans in the 12th century. As a result, the Welsh princes of Deheubarth (a former kingdom based in the southwest of Wales) transferred their patronage to the new abbey at Strata Florida, transforming it into the cultural and spiritual centre of the Welsh fight for independence. The abbey grounds claim to be the final resting place for no fewer than 11 Welsh princes, as well as the greatest of Welsh poets, Dafydd ap Gwilym (active in the 14th century). It was also in Strata Florida that *Brut y Tywysogion* (*Chronicle of the Princes*) was written, which is one of the most important primary sources for medieval Welsh history.

Unfortunately, this once splendid abbey is now in an extremely ruinous state, and compares unfavourably with Wales' best-preserved monastic remains at Tintern. It is likely that Strata Florida paid the price for staunchly supporting Wales' native princes. The abbey was badly damaged during the final years of Welsh independence at the end of the 13th century and again during the Glyndŵr Rising (1400–15), when an English garrison was quartered there.

Between Tyncwm farm and Llyn Egnant, the walk route follows an ancient trackway known as the Monks' Trod. This was developed by Cistercian monks to connect Strata Florida with Abbeycwmhir in Powys, and rises above Tyncwm along the tumbling mountain stream of Nant Egnant. The path then runs along the shores of Llyn Egnant (now a road), where the monks farmed eels and trout for food.

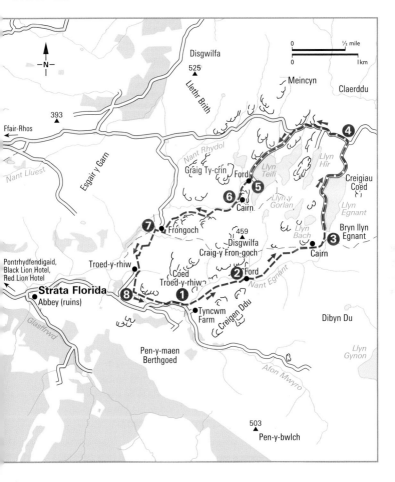

1. From the lay-by, walk back down the lane for a short distance to reach a bridleway sign by a bench. Turn right and follow an obvious path in the direction of Nant Egnant, a tumbling mountain stream that is crossed by a footbridge. Climb a steep bank ahead and turn left on to the track from Tyncwm farm.

2. Further up this beautiful rocky valley, Nant Egnant is crossed once again, this time by a ford. Continue through a gate, following the obvious path ever higher up the mountain. Not far past a cairn, the path bears left round a corner, and Llyn Egnant appears suddenly before you.

3. Pass through a gate and continue across a short boggy section towards the lake. Join a metalled track alongside the dam and follow this along the left-hand shore of the lake. Beyond Llyn Egnant, the track climbs to reach a T-junction with a narrow, unfenced lane.

4. Turn left and follow this winding, undulating lane for just over 0.5 miles (800m). Take the second vehicle track on the left, which crosses more open moorland towards the largest of the lakes, Llyn Teifi. Continue along the right-hand edge of the lake to a dam.

5. Where progress is blocked by a rusty iron gate, join a narrow path to the right of a fence and track. At the end of the fence, the path bears slightly right, winding its way down a valley to a stile. Cross over and ford a stream (the infant Afon Teifi). Bear right and follow the river downstream.

6. The valley opens out near a stone cairn. Continue downstream, now with a fence between the path and the river. Where the stream comes back under the fence, bear left to pick up a path higher up the valley slope. Go through a wooden gate and follow a clear path curving left round the hill towards Frongoch farm.

7. Bear right in front of the abandoned farmhouse and follow the farm track down to the next house along, Troed-y-rhiw. With the house on your immediate right, bear left through a gateway and continue along the bottom edge of a field, with the hedge to your right.

8. At the end of the field, the path joins a narrow ledge as it curves left across a steep, open slope. Descend obliquely down the hill to rejoin the lane from Strata Florida. Keep ahead up the valley to return to the lay-by.

Where to eat and drink

There's not a great deal of choice locally, as might be expected from the remoteness of the area. Like many small Welsh towns, Pontrhydfendigaid is home to a Black Lion and a Red Lion, both of which offer excellent pub food and a good selection of ales.

What to see

The steep, bracken-covered slopes to the southeast of Troed-y-rhiw farm were once clothed in Welsh oak trees. Much of this timber would have been harvested by the monks at Strata Florida to be used for building. There are only a few scattered trees left today, but the area is still known in Welsh as Coed Troed-y-rhiw ('Troed-y-rhiw Wood').

While you're there

A visit to Strata Florida is a must. There is not a great deal left of the original abbey, but detailed information boards give an excellent idea of what the site would have looked like in its heyday and how the monks who lived there helped shape the valley. Look up and you will see the 13ft (4m) sculpture of a medieval pilgrim cresting the skyline.

INTO CWM RHEIDOL FROM DEVIL'S BRIDGE

DISTANCE/TIME	7 miles (11.3km) / 3hrs 30min
ASCENT/GRADIENT	1,500ft (460m) / ▲ ▲ ▲
PATHS	Well-marked field and woodland paths across some steep, rough terrain (19 stiles)
LANDSCAPE	Wooded river valleys and upland pasture
SUGGESTED MAP	OS Explorer 213 Aberystwyth & Cwm Rheidol
START/FINISH	Grid reference: SN739768
DOG FRIENDLINESS	Dogs need to be kept under close control near fast-flowing rivers and fields with sheep
PARKING	Car park opposite the terminus for the Vale of Rheidol Railway
PUBLIC TOILETS	At the car park in Devil's Bridge (open Easter to end of September)
NOTES	Care needs to be taken where the path is narrow and exposed

The immediate neighbourhood of Devil's Bridge contains some of the most spectacular scenery in mid Wales. The village itself is bisected by the Mynach river, a tributary of the Rheidol, which plunges some 300ft (90m) down five great rocky steps into the Rheidol Valley. Crossing the river's deep, narrow ravine are three bridges (c. 1188, 1753, 1901), unusually built one on top of the other. According to local legend, the oldest of the bridges was built by the Devil himself, though it is more likely to have been built by the monks of Strata Florida. The name of the village in Welsh, Pontarfynach, translates as 'Bridge on [the] Monk'.

Below Devil's Bridge, the land falls steeply away into Cwm Rheidol. The valley slopes are clothed in ancient oak woodland and are a designated national nature reserve (Coed Rheidol). The moist, shady conditions provide an ideal environment for mosses, liverworts and lichens, which carpet the steep rocky slopes near the bottom of the gorge. These in turn support a varied ecosystem, with nearly 80 species of birds having been recorded in the woodland. Breeding birds include the redstart, the wood warbler and the pied flycatcher. Otters are known to live in the river, but you'll be lucky to spot one.

Between Ponterwyd and Devil's Bridge, the Rheidol is squeezed through a narrow, rocky ravine culminating in the Gyfarllwyd Falls, 'a valley within a valley' formed as a result of headward erosion during the last ice age. Unfortunately, the deep gorge is almost entirely inaccessible to walkers, though the crossing of Parson's Bridge near Ysbyty Cynfyn provides a brief but memorable glimpse of this extraordinary landscape. Lead mining in the valley was an important industry up until the end of the 19th century, and it has left a legacy of serious environmental problems in the Rheidol river. These include elevated levels of zinc, lead, copper, cadmium and other metals, as well as high levels of acidity. Artificial wetlands have been created downstream from Devil's Bridge to act as a biofilter, removing pollutants and contaminated sediments from the water.

Winding across the wooded slopes between Aberystwyth and Devil's Bridge is the Vale of Rheidol Railway. This narrow-gauge steam line was opened in 1902, principally to serve the logging and mining industries in the valley. To save money, rock was hand-hewn out of the steep valley slopes rather than blasted. By the time the railway opened, however, the lead-mining industry was in a steep decline, and tourism rapidly became a more important source of income for the railway. The line continues to offer a regular service between May and the end of October each year.

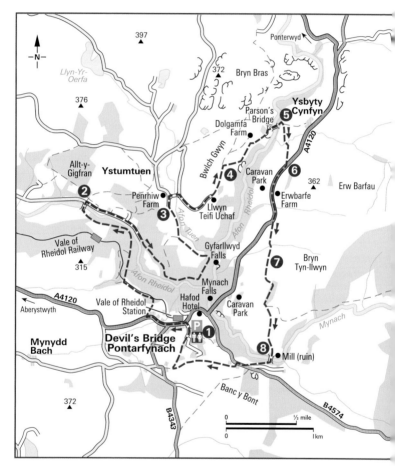

1. From the car park, return to the main road and turn left. Just past the last house, take a path on the right signed to Borth. This runs above the Vale of Rheidol Railway, then crosses the line and continues down through woodland to a bridge over the Afon Rheidol.

2. Turn right and follow a lane/track up the valley to a sharp left-hand bend. Keep ahead on to a footpath, then turn steeply uphill to the left and climb

through woodland. On emerging in a field, climb again, then join a level grassy track parallel to a wooded valley on the right.

3. At a metal gate, keep ahead on to a vehicle track as far as Penrhiw farm. Turn right at a footpath sign and cross a field to a footbridge over the Afon Tuen. Climb to a lane and turn right. Pass a farm (Llwyn Teifi Uchaf) and continue on to a level farm track.

4. Where directed, fork right on to a grassy track and descend gently to a stone ruin. Cross a stile and descend along the right-hand field edge to another stile. Keep ahead to a stile near Dolgamfa farm, then descend to the right along a path between fences. Bear left and follow a woodland path down to Parson's Bridge.

5. Cross the Afon Rheidol and climb steeply left. Hairpin right, then, at the next hairpin bend, keep ahead along a rough, narrow path to a stile into a field. Following waymark arrows, cross two fields to reach a footbridge over a stream, then keep ahead through two more fields to a junction with the A4120.

6. Turn right and follow the road past Erwbarfe farm and caravan park. At the second lay-by on the left, cross the road to a stile and bear right towards the top corner of a field. Cross a stile near a clump of trees and climb left to another. Turn right along a level grassy track towards a field gate.

7. After a second field gate, leave the track for a waymarked path bearing left. Climb towards trees and follow the woodland boundary to the right. At a gravel track, keep ahead on to a rougher track alongside a fence. Head straight down a field to an enclosed path and descend to the ruins of a mill by the Mynach river.

8. Cross a bridge and climb steeply to a road. Turn right, then bear left towards a house. Climb steps to a stile and join a sunken track. In an area of Scots pine, turn right at a waymark post and cross a field. Climb a stile in a fence and follow a downhill track back to the car park.

Where to eat and drink
There are a number of cafés and tea rooms in Devil's Bridge, but if you want something a little stronger, you will need to head down to the Hafod Hotel. The restaurant serves a good selection (vegetarian, vegan and gluten free options are available) from an a la carte menu as well as ciabattas, wraps and takeaway foods.

What to see
The oak woodlands of Cwm Rheidol are comprised predominantly of sessile oak trees, which unlike the closely related English oak possess stalked leaves and stalkless (sessile) acorns. They flourish best in the wetter, upland areas of Britain along the Atlantic fringe, and have been designated the national tree of both Wales and Cornwall.

While you're there
No trip to Devil's Bridge is complete without a walk round the spectacular Mynach Falls. The longer of the two circular trails (privately owned and maintained and there is an admission fee to walk either trail) drops down 100 continuous steps to the base of the falls in a peaceful wooded gorge.

26

BELOW THE BLACK MOUNTAINS ESCARPMENT

DISTANCE/TIME	8 miles (12.9km) / 3hrs 30min
ASCENT/GRADIENT	1,060ft (320m) / ▲ ▲
PATHS	Roads, tracks, field paths; nature reserve trails muddy and slippery in winter (20 stiles)
LANDSCAPE	Market town, river gorge, woodland, common, upland pasture
SUGGESTED MAP	OS Explorer OL13 Brecon Beacons National Park
START/FINISH	Grid reference: SO152336
DOG FRIENDLINESS	Lots of fields with sheep and occasionally cattle – keep dogs on a lead
PARKING	Large car park on the southwestern edge of Talgarth, just off the A479
PUBLIC TOILETS	In centre of Talgarth
NOTES	Paths in Pwll-y-wrach Nature Reserve can be very muddy and slippery in winter. To avoid the worst of the mud, continue up the lane (at Point 2) and join an easy access trail from a car parking area on the right.

Talgarth is one of the prettiest small towns in Wales, a pleasant and fascinating place to wander around. The beginning and end of this walk take in the best bits, including the attractive parish church dedicated to one of King Brychan of Brycheiniog's many daughters. The remainder of the walk explores the area of land rising from Talgarth towards the Black Mountains' northern escarpment. This varied mix of woodland, common and upland pasture provides many miles of rewarding walking, as well as excellent views of the escarpment. Do not expect to encounter crowds of walkers: this quiet, peaceful area is often neglected by visitors to the national park.

A highlight of the first half of the walk is Pwll-y-wrach, a nature reserve comprising a remnant of ancient woodland in a steep-sloped valley along the River Ennig. The damp, humid woods provide food and shelter for a wide variety of plants, fungi and animals, including a significant population of resident dormice. Otters are known to hunt in the river, which also attracts a number of different bird species. You may spot a pied flycatcher or dipper feeding on the insects that live in and around the water.

At the eastern end of the reserve, an impressive waterfall tumbles into a dark pool – the 'witch's pool' from which the reserve derives its name. The pool has a wild, haunted feel and features in a number of local legends. King Brychan's daughter St Gwendoline is reputed to have bathed in the pool (a story which makes her sound more like a Celtic goddess than an early Christian saint), and there's a popular myth that the pool was used to duck suspected witches.

The flat grassland to the east of Llanelieu is part of an enclosed common called Rhos Fawr. This was land over which local farmers had common rights, allowing them to graze livestock. Those with no land of their own relied on common land to feed the small number of animals they kept. Disputes and numbers were regulated by manorial courts to prevent overgrazing.

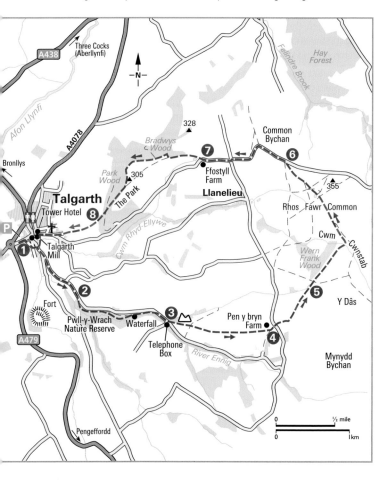

1. Turn left out of the car park walking towards the town centre. Take the next road on the right ('Heol Las'). Turn right at a T-junction and then left down a tarmac path ('Pwll-y-Wrach'). Follow the River Ennig to a road and turn right. Cross the river and continue ahead up Hospital Road.

2. Where the gradient steepens ahead, fork right into Pwll-y-wrach Nature Reserve and take the path descending right. Drop to the river and follow the waymarked path upstream to the main waterfall. Climb steps to a gate and continue ahead along the river. Rejoin the lane and turn right.

3. At a red telephone box, bear left over a stile. Turn left at a rough track and emerge in a field. Climb steeply, then keep ahead to pass through a succession of smaller fields. Keep ahead to a gap in a hedge, then follow the left-hand edge of fields as far as Pen y bryn farm.

4. Bear left at a waymark post to meet a lane. Cross to a track opposite and climb on to the common. Turn left, continuing straight ahead where the common boundary drops away. Pick up a path through gorse bushes and shortly arrive at a small wooden gate in a fence.

5. Go through the gate and follow the path along the edge of Wern Frank Wood. After crossing the stream in Cwm Cwnstab, take an obvious grassy path bearing left. Descend across the middle of Rhos Fawr Common, aiming for the right-hand end of a small, shallow pool. Keep ahead to an unfenced lane in the common's northwest corner.

6. Turn left along the lane, passing through a gate. Follow the road round a left-hand bend on Common Bychan and then through a second gate. Take the right-hand lane at a fork and head gently downhill towards the farm buildings of Ffostyll. Bear right at a footpath sign in front of the farmhouse.

7. Follow a muddy track to a field and bear left along a clear grassy path. The right of way climbs through a copse, then continues along the right-hand edge of fields. Eventually, cross a stile into Park Wood (ignore an earlier stile into Bradwys Wood) and join a narrow path descending obliquely left. Cross a wide track and continue down to a stile into a field.

8. Keep straight down the field and along the left-hand edge of two further fields. Follow a tarmac lane down to Church Street and turn right. Pass by St Gwendoline's Church, turn left on to Brook Lane and descend to a stream. Cross over and follow a tarmac path up to a road. Turn right and retrace your outward route through Talgarth.

Where to eat and drink

The centre of Talgarth contains two pubs and a café. The Bridge End Inn is cosy, but lacks the Tower Hotel's range of award-winning ciders. The Strand Bookshop and café offers a wide range of foods from breakfast and sandwiches to main meals and hot drinks. There's also an excellent Cantonese takeaway.

What to see

In March and early April, you may notice a field of daffodils on the mountain above Pen y bryn. These are farmed for their galantamine, a compound that slows the progression of Alzheimer's disease. Daffodils grown in Wales contain greater concentrations of galantimine than those grown in drier areas of the UK.

While you're there

Talgarth Mill is a newly restored 18th-century mill in the heart of the town. Powered by water from the River Ellywe, the mill now operates as a community-run flour mill and traditional bakery, using local organic herbs and beer to bake its speciality loaves. You can take a guided tour of the mill and even learn some useful bread-making techniques.

27

CAPEL-Y-FFIN
AND LLANTHONY

DISTANCE/TIME	9.5 miles (15.3km) / 5hrs 30min
ASCENT/GRADIENT	2,460ft (750m) / ▲ ▲ ▲
PATHS	Easy-to-follow paths, steep slopes, open moorland, muddy lowland trails, many stiles
LANDSCAPE	Classic U-shaped valleys topped with broad heather-strewn moorland
SUGGESTED MAP	OS Explorer OL13 Brecon Beacons National Park
START/FINISH	Grid reference: SO255314
DOG FRIENDLINESS	Some difficult stiles, care needed near livestock, no dogs in grounds of priory
PARKING	Narrow pull-in at southern edge of Capel-y-ffin, close to bridge
PUBLIC TOILETS	Next to Llanthony Priory

The sheer size of the Vale of Ewyas means that it's best explored in two different walks. The northern reaches are crossed in Walk 28, while this one tracks south from Capel-y-ffin to loop around the tiny settlement of Llanthony. This circuit has the added advantage of passing the ruins of Llanthony Priory and the opportunity of a great pub at the half-way stage. The down side is that the head of the valley is some way to the north so, in order to follow both ridges, you'll have to drop into the foot of the valley and then climb out again.

The early stages of both walks follow the same line as far as the crest of the Ffawyddog ridge. From here, this circuit will take you south, over the distinctive serrated skyline of Chwarel y Fan, the site of some disused quarries and, at 2,227ft (679m), the highest point of the day. The ridge then drops steadily down to Bal-Mawr, where you'll follow the banks of the Bwchel brook, through Cwm Bwchel, to the hamlet of Llanthony. From the priory, it's up again, easily at first as you cross the fields adjacent to the ruins, but then steeply to gain a blunt spur that leads on to the slim ridge of Hatterrall. Offa's Dyke Path follows the crest of the ridge, as does the border. Another steep drop brings you back to the pastures above Capel-y-ffin, where you'll pass two tiny, whitewashed chapels before you reach the road.

In an attempt to keep the Welsh to the west, King Offa, the 8th-century ruler of Mercia (Central England), decided to mark out his borders using a deep ditch and an earth wall to strengthen any natural boundaries such as rivers or ridges. It ran from Prestatyn, on the north coast of Wales, to Chepstow, at the mouth of the River Wye. In places, it was over 20ft (6m) high and 60ft (18m) wide. Although the official border has changed a little in the ensuing years, it still follows a similar line to the original earthworks. Offa's Dyke National Trail opened in 1971. It follows the north–south line of the dyke for 177 miles (285km) and showcases the incredible diversity of the Welsh countryside.

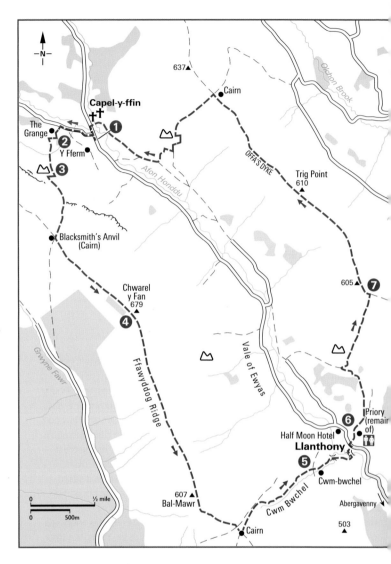

1. Walk towards the bridge, but before you cross it, bear left up a narrow lane, signposted to The Grange Pony Trekking Centre. Follow this along the side of the stream and past a footpath on the left, marked by a stone archway. Continue to a drive on the left, again leading to the trekking centre, and follow this up to a cluster of barns.

2. Keep right here and continue uphill to a large house on the right, with a gate blocking your progress ahead. Bear around to the left and climb on a loose rocky track that leads up to another gate. Pass through this and follow a rough, eroded track as it zig-zags up on to easier ground. Cross the source of a small stream, and continue to the foot of a steep zig-zag track that climbs steeply up the escarpment.

3. Follow this, bearing both right and left and then, as the gradient eases, continue ahead on a broad and often boggy track. Take this past a few small cairns to a large one, the Blacksmith's Anvil, that sits on top of the ridge. Turn left here and continue to follow the track south over Chwarel y Fan.

4. Walk straight on, along the line of the ridge, to reach the summit of Bal-Mawr. Carrying on the same track, go down to the left and pass a good track on your left-hand side. Keep ahead to a cairn and then descend to the left. Drop to a fork where you keep right to follow the brook to a crossroads of paths. Maintain your direction (signposted 'Cwm Bwchel').

5. Cross a stile, down past a house, and over another stile. Ignore another stile on the right and continue down to another at the bottom of the field. Cross this and bear right to cross another and a footbridge. Keep walking straight ahead to another stile and then continue to a gate. Go immediately through a small metal gate and follow the stream down through another gate to another footbridge. Cross this and take the lane to the road. Turn left here, then turn right to visit the priory.

6. Go through a gate on the left, in front of the priory (signposted to Hatterrall Hill), and follow the main track to a stream, where you turn left to a gate. Continue through a succession of fields, over two stiles and a small copse. Follow the path up on to the ridge and continue to a T-junction; Offa's Dyke is where you turn left.

7. Walk along Offa's Dyke, pass the trig point and continue for another mile (1.6km) to a cairn and a marker stone at a crossroads of paths. Turn left and follow the path down around a sharp left-right zig-zag to a fence. Turn right here, then turn left over a stile. Walk down, over another stile to a hedge at the bottom of the next field, cross another stile and carry on down, before bearing right, crossing a stream and turning left to pass over a stile and onwards onto a tarmac lane. Turn right through a gate and follow this through a yard, where it becomes a rough track. Keep ahead to a sharp left-hand bend and keep straight ahead, up steps and over a stile. Continue straight ahead through more fields to join another lane and follow this down, past two chapels to the road. Turn left to return to your car.

Where to eat and drink

The Half Moon Hotel in Llanthony is worth a visit. This traditional pub, popular with walkers, serves excellent food and offers a good choice of beers. It's at the half-way point of the walk, just past the entrance of Llanthony Priory, or on the way back down the valley at the end of the day.

What to see

Worship at Llanthony Priory dates back to the 6th century AD, when St David himself founded a chapel. The remaining building that you see today was constructed in the 12th century as a religious sanctuary for the Norman knight William de Lacey. J M W Turner painted the ruins from the opposite hillside.

AROUND THE VALE OF EWYAS

DISTANCE/TIME	9 miles (14.5km) / 4hrs
ASCENT/GRADIENT	1,560ft (475m) / ▲ ▲ ▲
PATHS	Easy-to-follow tracks, steep slopes, open moorland
LANDSCAPE	Classic U-shaped valleys, broad heather-strewn moorland
SUGGESTED MAP	OS Explorer OL13 Brecon Beacons National Park
START/FINISH	Grid reference: SO255314
DOG FRIENDLINESS	Great for dogs but care required near livestock
PARKING	Narrow pull-in at southern edge of village, close to bridge
PUBLIC TOILETS	None on route

The steep clamber up out of Capel-y-ffin will definitely have you trying to catch your breath, but don't be put off. Once you've made the giant cairn that marks the top, the rest is child's play and the views, as you cruise comfortably along the giant whaleback that makes up the Ffawyddog ridge, are just superb. At Pen Rhos Dirion, you nudge over 2,296ft (700m) and reap the fruits of your labour with a sweeping panorama over the Wye Valley.

East is Twmpa, often referred to as 'Lord Hereford's Knob', and beyond that, the Gospel Pass and Hay Bluff – the eastern end of the impressive Black Mountains escarpment. The head of the Ewyas Valley is split in two by a rugged slither of upland known as Darren Llwyd. This offers an airy return route with views to the east that match the earlier vista to the west. The spur drops away sharply at its southern tip and your eyes will be drawn straight ahead, where the Ewyas displays the classic U-shape of its ice-age roots.

This walk is near to the small town of Hay-on-Wye, a bustling, cosmopolitan place, which can be seen clearly from the northern escarpment. The town marks both the northernmost point of the National Park and also the Anglo-Welsh border, with Herefordshire to the east and Powys to the west. Like many of the towns in the area, Hay-on-Wye grew up around its impressive Norman castle, which was built on the site of an earlier motte-and-bailey construction. These days, the town is known as the 'second-hand book capital of Wales', and for the Hay Festival of Literature and Arts, better known as the Hay Festival, celebrated every year in late spring.

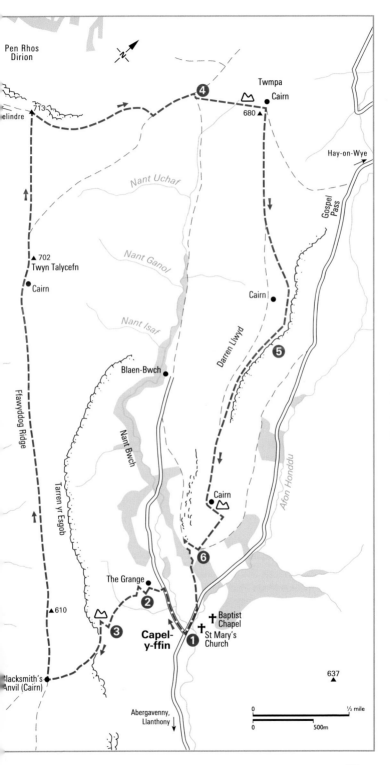

Pen Rhos
Dirion

Twmpa
Cairn

4

680 ▲

Hay-on-Wye

713
elindre

Nant Uchaf

Gospel
Pass

Nant Ganol

▲ 702
Twyn Talycefn

Cairn

Nant Isaf

Cairn

Darren Llwyd

5

Ffawyddog Ridge

Blaen-Bwch

Afon Honddu

Tarren yr Esgob

Nant Bwch

Cairn

▲ 610

Cairn

6

The Grange

2

Baptist
Chapel

3

**Capel-
y-ffin**

1

St Mary's
Church

Blacksmith's
Anvil (Cairn)

637 ▲

0   ½ mile

Abergavenny,
Llanthony ↓

0   500m

103

1. Walk towards the bridge, but before you cross it, bear left up a narrow lane, signposted to The Grange Pony Trekking Centre. Follow this along the side of the stream and past a footpath on the left, marked by a stone archway. Continue to a drive on the left, again leading to the trekking centre, and follow this up to a cluster of barns.

2. Keep right here and continue uphill to a large house on the right, with a gate blocking your progress ahead. Bear around to the left and climb on a loose rocky track that leads up to another gate. Pass through this and follow a rough, eroded track as it zig-zags up on to easier ground. Cross the source of a small stream, and continue to the foot of a steep zig-zag track that climbs steeply up the escarpment.

3. Follow this, bearing both right and left and then, as the gradient eases, continue ahead on a broad and often boggy track. Take this past a few small cairns to a large one that sits on top of the rounded ridge. Turn right and follow the track easily over Twyn Talycefn to the trig point on Pen Rhos Dirion. (The summit can be avoided by a clear path that traverses right before the final climb.) Turn right and drop steeply down through the heather into a broad saddle.

4. Keep straight ahead over the flat section and then climb steeply up on to Twmpa. Turn right here and then, for maximum effect, bear left on to a narrower track that follows the line of the east-facing escarpment. Stay with this track until the ridge narrows and drops steeply away.

5. Descend directly to a large square cairn, then keep ahead to continue down a steep spur and as it becomes too steep to continue, zig-zag left then right, to cut a steep line through the bracken to a junction with a broad contouring bridleway. Keep straight ahead to cross this and drop down to pick up a narrow stony track that runs along the side of a wood.

6. After the wood, ignore a grassy path that crosses obliquely. Shortly after, turn left almost back on yourself to follow this down to a stile and keep straight ahead to pass between two houses. When you reach the drive, keep straight ahead to cross a stile and continue in the same direction to cross another stile in the bottom corner. Turn right to follow the lane to return to your car.

Where to eat and drink

You'll find the Three Horsehoes in Felindre, which is well known for its cosy cottage appeal and good food and drink. Or, while heading south, there's the Half Moon Hotel in Llanthony village, which is a walker's favourite, serving real ale and offering excellent pub food.

What to see

The tiny chapel that you pass at the end of the walk is St Mary's Church, one of the smallest in the country, with an interior that measures only 26ft (7.9m) by 13ft (3.9m). It was built in 1762, and the porch was added 55 years later. There are galleries along the west and south walls and an octagonal pulpit. The belfry, which is decidedly lopsided, houses two bells. In recent years, the simple architecture of Welsh chapels has finally become recognised as a significant aspect of the Welsh culture.

WAUN FACH FROM THE GRWYN FAWR VALLEY

DISTANCE/TIME	9.25 miles (14.9km) / 4hrs
ASCENT/GRADIENT	2,000ft (610m) / ▲ ▲ ▲
PATHS	Clear tracks over open moorland, one indistinct path over boggy ground, steep descent
LANDSCAPE	Rolling moorland, deep valleys
SUGGESTED MAP	OS Explorer OL13 Brecon Beacons National Park
START/FINISH	Grid reference: SO253285
DOG FRIENDLINESS	Care needed near sheep
PARKING	Car park at head of lane at start
PUBLIC TOILETS	None on route
NOTES	Difficult navigation in poor visibility

The high ground of the Black Mountains consists of a 1-mile (1.6km) long, blunt and boggy ridge that runs between the two high points of Waun Fach and Pen y Gadair Fawr. Waun Fach sneaks the gold medal for altitude; at 2,661ft (811m), it stands a less than obvious 36ft (11m) above its shapelier neighbour. But erosion and time has reduced its lofty summit plateau to little more than a shallow peaty scoop that houses the stranded base of a long removed triangulation pillar. This has left the distinctive, conical summit of Pen y Gadair Fawr as the far more worthwhile objective. It's dry, offers great views over the Grwyne Fechan Valley and even comes complete with a tumbledown windbreak, next to the summit cairn.

The real beauty of this small cluster of rounded peaks are the valleys that drop away dramatically to either side of the ridge. The Grwyne Fechan Valley, on the western side, is the wilder and more picturesque of the two. It has no road access and its tiny brook is almost permanently in the shadow of the string of imposing peaks that define its western banks.

The valley of Grwyne Fawr is the larger, however (Fawr means large or great). Its windswept rolling moorland cradles a large reservoir that provides a scenic focal point for walkers and sightseers alike. It's fed by the tumbling Grwyne Fawr river, a typical fast-flowing mountain stream that rises out of the boggy plateau at its head. The easy angle of the valley means that its grassy floor, penetrated by a good track for most of its length, offers a gentle knee-up on to the higher ground and this provides the easiest approach to most of the surrounding peaks. Lower down the valley, beneath the reservoir, the walls steepen and their wooded slopes provide a short but extremely sharp exit from the lofty flanks of Pen y Gadair Fawr.

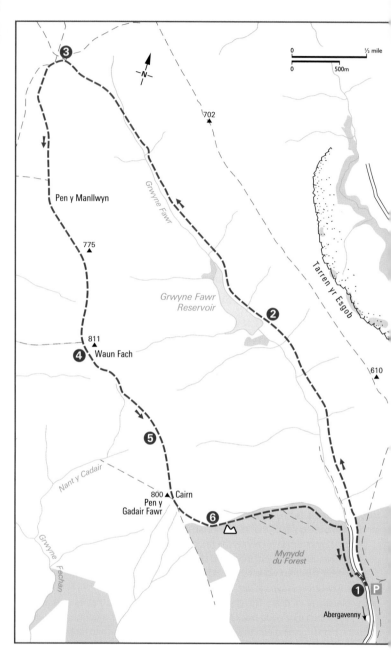

1. Take the broad track at the far end of the car park and follow it out on to the road. Turn right to continue up the valley then, after about 30yds (27m), fork right on to a stony track that runs along the bottom of the forest. Follow this track ignoring a fork off to right and continue through two gates to a third gate, by a stand of trees, situated above the Grwyne Fawr Reservoir.

2. Keeping the trees to your left, carry on past the reservoir and up the valley. Go through another gate and continue until the track finally fords the Grwyne Fawr stream. Stay on the stony track, which now peters out to become grassy for a while before deepening into an obvious rut. Continue on to the flat ground above the steep northern escarpment, where the path meets a fence by a stile on your right.

3. Turn left on to a clear track and then, after 100yds (91m), turn left again by a tiny cairn on to a faint grassy track that leads up the front of a blunt spur. Follow this over numerous peaty hollows to the summit plateau of Waun Fach, easily identified by a large concrete block.

4. Continue on in the same direction (southeast) across a large expanse of boggy ground. There's no clear path on this section, but there are usually plenty of footprints in the wet ground leading towards the obvious cairn-topped peak of Pen y Gadair Fawr, at the far end of the ridge. In the saddle between the two summits, you'll pick up a faint path that initially follows the eroded line of a stream.

5. The path improves as it continues, eventually leaving the stream behind and making a beeline for the peak ahead. Climb to the cairn, then continue in the same direction to drop steeply. Here you are faced with a plethora of unhelpfully brief paths vying for your attention. Take one of the middle ones, heading southeast towards what was the edge of the forest. Most of the trees have been harvested here, leaving rows of stumps. Make your way to the fence at the edge of the forested area and turn left along it.

6. Take particular care here because the path drops steeply down the hillside as it hugs the fence to its right. The path follows the fence all the way down to the river, crossing a stream on the way. At the river, turn right. Continue along the river bank for about 400yds (366m), then cross the bridge to the road. Turn right on to this to return to the car park.

Where to eat and drink
This is a pretty remote area but The Skirrid Inn, in Llanvihangel Crucorney, just off the A465, between Abergavenny and Hereford, is reputed to be the oldest pub in Wales and is certainly worth a visit for a drink or a meal. Alternatively, head back down the A465 to Abergavenny where there's plenty of choice.

What to see
On the walk up to Waun Fach, you'll pass a succession of deep trenches in the grass-topped peat. These are known as peat hags and appear all over the National Park. In some areas, geological movements have brought the peat to the surface where it forms bogs that have gradually dried out over thousands of years. The surfaces of these bogs are easily eroded and the action of running water combined with frost, ice, snow and very high winds has carved out deep trenches. In some places they can be up to 10ft (3m) deep. This type of peat is burnt as fuel, but there's no evidence of domestic peat cutting in this area. The acidic nature of this type of soil supports a variety of plant life including heather and bilberry.

THE CREST OF Y GRIB

DISTANCE/TIME	8 miles (12.9km) / 4hrs 30min
ASCENT/GRADIENT	1,906ft (581m) / ▲ ▲ ▲
PATHS	Clear tracks over farmland, rolling moorland and narrow ridge, quiet lane, several stiles
LANDSCAPE	High mountain plateau, narrow ridge, steep grassy escarpment, deep and remote cwms
SUGGESTED MAP	OS Explorer OL13 Brecon Beacons National Park
START/FINISH	Grid reference: SO175295
DOG FRIENDLINESS	Care needed near livestock
PARKING	Dinas Castle Inn, Pengenffordd, allows parking for small fee
PUBLIC TOILETS	None on route

This is the classic climb on to the highest ground of the Black Mountains. The steep western slopes of the towering massif, accentuated by a succession of grassy arêtes (narrow ridges) and rounded promontories, hide a multitude of remote cwms (steep-sided hollows at the head of a valley or on a mountainside) that rarely reveal their splendour to the walker.

At 1,476ft (450m) above sea level, Castell Dinas can safely claim to be the site of one of the highest castles in Britain. Sadly, only a few stones, scattered around the rocky hilltop, are left to tell the story. It's a stunning viewpoint and, courtesy of the recently instated permissive path that leads from Pengenffordd to its crown, it adds considerable interest to this excellent high mountain walk.

From the airy ramparts of Castell Dinas, the full length of the bold escarpment unfolds and, while many paths breach its defences, none do so in quite such a dramatic fashion as the one that traces the slender crest of Y Grib. Compared to the gentle standards of this normally rounded and uniform landscape, this narrow grassy walkway feels almost knife-edge in places. Once up, you'll make easy progress through the eroded peat of Pen y Manllwyn and across the top of the boggy plateau to the massif's high point of Waun Fach.

The line of descent harbours its own treasures as it follows the narrow spur of Pen Trumau, which sweeps gracefully around a deep chasm formed by the infant Grwyne Fechan river. Huge views across the valley show the formidable bulk of Waun Fach as it would want to be seen; the usually understated summit transforms itself into an impressive towering giant that stands head and shoulders above the line of pretenders to its grassy crown. A rocky saddle, steeped in the atmosphere of the craggy peaks that surround it, marks the last of the high mountain scenery.

A basic windbreak offers shelter from the cruel wind that often sweeps through the pass and also affords fine views over the expansive Grwyne Fechan Valley. The route is for more experienced walkers, and should be not attempted in poor weather or when visibility is reduced.

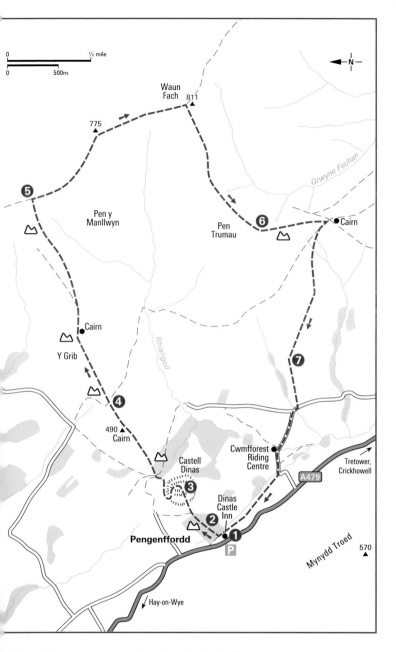

1. A set of wooden steps go down from the back of the car park on the eastern side of the road. These lead on to a rough track where you turn right and then, after 30yds (27m), left over a stile. Follow the permissive path down the side of the wood to a stream, cross a stile and then cross the stream.

2. Keep to the left edge of the field, with trees on your left, and climb steeply to the top of the field. Leave the wood behind and follow the fence line upwards to another stile. This leads on to the flanks of Castell Dinas.

3. Keep straight ahead here to cross the ruins and descend steeply into a deep saddle. Cross a stile and a broad track, then climb directly up the steep spur ahead. You're now on Y Grib and it's possible to follow the faint track all the way up to a cairn and then down to a small notch where your route is crossed by a bridleway.

4. Climb steeply back out of this and hug the crest up to another cairn. Now keep ahead on a fainter path that passes another cairn before climbing steeply, straight ahead, on to the broad spur of Pen y Manllwyn.

5. Here, at a tiny cairn, turn right on to a clear track that leads over the top of Pen y Manllwyn (marked by a cairn) and up to the boggy plateau on top of Waun Fach. The summit is stranded in a puddle of wet peat that makes it an undesirable picnic spot. Turn right and follow the obvious path down on to the ever-narrowing spur of Pen Trumau.

6. Cross the narrow summit and, as the ground steepens, follow the path through rocky outcrops to a broad saddle, marked by a large cairn. Turn sharp right here and follow the main track as it descends, easily at first. This steepens and becomes rocky for a while, going through several gates, before it reaches a gate above a walled track.

7. Follow the track down to the road and turn right, then immediately left. Drop to the bottom of the valley past Cwmfforest Riding Centre and climb out again on the other side. As the road turns sharply to the left, bear right on to a stony farm track that runs between hedgerows. Follow this track until it turns sharply left where you continue straight ahead along a narrower track between hedges. This will take you past the stile you crossed earlier, on the right-hand side, then take the steps on your left, back to the car park.

Where to eat and drink

The Dinas Castle Inn has long been a centre for walkers, serving great food and a choice of ales. Dogs are not allowed inside, but there is a special children's menu and extra large portions are available for hungry hikers. The inn also offers bed and breakfast and low-cost bunkhouse accommodation for groups.

While you're there

The Normans finally settled on Tretower for their best defence of the pass and in the 13th century, built a basic round tower on the site of an earlier fortification. The tower wasn't as successful as its owners had hoped and it nearly fell to both Llywelyn the Last in the late 13th century and again in the 14th century. The original tower, together with a 15th-century mansion built during more peaceful times, and some glorious gardens are all open to the public.

AROUND LLANGORSE LAKE

DISTANCE/TIME	3 miles (4.8km) / 1hr 30min
ASCENT/GRADIENT	100ft (30m)
PATHS	Footpaths over agricultural land and short road section, several stiles
LANDSCAPE	Marshy lakeside surrounded by mountains
SUGGESTED MAP	OS Explorer OL13 Brecon Beacons National Park
START/FINISH	Grid reference: SO128272
DOG FRIENDLINESS	Awkward stiles, care needed near livestock and wildfowl
PARKING	At Llangorse Lake
PUBLIC TOILETS	At start
NOTES	In particularly wet periods the Afon Llynfi is liable to burst its banks, making the start of this walk impassable

This walk is a gentle tramp around the lush meadows that hold South Wales' largest natural lake, Llangorse. The lake perches on the watershed between the Usk to the south and the Wye, which runs north of the Black Mountains. It's well known for its ecology and particularly its birdlife, which is protected by a nature reserve on the southern shores. The water attracts a huge number of wintering birds, as well as acting as a stop-off for species that migrate. The reeds lining the lake also provide an important habitat: a dragonfly known as *Ischnura pumilio*, is thought to breed only in one other spot in the UK.

On the lake, you'll find the only known crannog (manmade island) in all of Wales – and there are none at all in England. Tree-ring dating of the Llangorse crannog has established that it was put together in several stages between 889 and 893 AD. However, it didn't last long, being destroyed by fire in 916. The Anglo-Saxon Chronicle appears to reveal how this came to pass: 'Æthelflæd ['The Lady of the Mercians'] sent an army into Wales and stormed Brecenanmere [Llangorse Lake] and there captured the wife of the king and thirty-three other persons.' It's not beyond the realms of imagination that they set light to the island afterwards. Although it's not possible to visit the crannog as it is too fragile, it is possible to give it a close inspection by hiring a rowing boat or kayak at the lakeside and circumnavigating it. A modern replica crannog, a short distance away, is filled with information and stories about the crannog and the lake that surrounds it.

Several tales have attached themselves to the Lake. The chronicler Giraldus Cambrensis (Gerald of Wales), who visited in 1188, wrote that local people had reported the water turning green – a portent of impending invasion – and that sometimes this was accompanied by scarlet streaks in the water 'as if blood were flowing along certain currents and eddies'. These are now thought to have been caused by algal blooms or sediments.

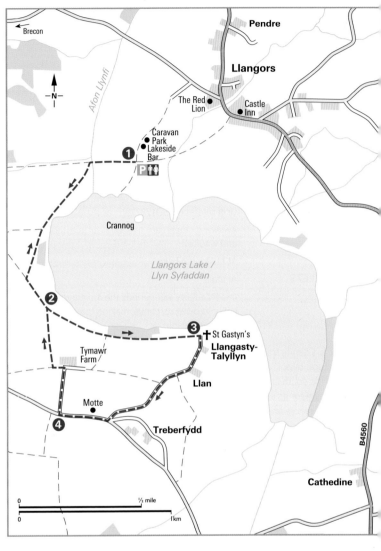

1. From the car park next to the toilets, walk across the access road and continue straight across the Common on a grassy track. This leads to a small footbridge over the Afon Llynfi. Cross the bridge and bear diagonally left to cross the centre of the field towards another small footbridge and stile. Although you are on level ground, the walk has great views over some of the surrounding peaks and on this stretch you'll see the sloping table top of Pen y Fan clearly ahead in the distance. Continue in the same direction across the next field until you come to a stone wall, which is vaulted by a step stile. Cross this and maintain the same direction. You'll notice a small copse on your left-hand side and beyond this a dense patch of reeds. At the end of this field, you come to a wooden footbridge. Cross this and the stile to continue in the same direction again. This leads on to a short boardwalk that takes you through a small gate. Keep straight ahead here, to the left-hand edge of the field.

2. Pass through another gate to continue along the same line. At the end of this field, pass through another gate and join a broad grassy track at a junction. This is Llangasty Nature Reserve and if you turn left here, you'll come to a hide on your left-hand side. To continue, keep straight ahead, passing through a wide gate with two waymarkers on it. Keep left to walk above a small wood and then, at the end of the wood, bear around to the left on another boardwalk, which leads you to a kissing gate. Go into the wood and cross a footbridge to continue to another kissing gate. Keep ahead here, along the bottom of the field to another gate and maintain your direction to run along a scenic section of the lake shore – a great place to take a break. After passing a few lofty Scots pines you reach yet another gate, by the elegant 19th-century Church of St Gastyn's. This, along with the nearby school and manor house, were built by Robert Raikes, the originator of the Sunday School in Britain.

3. Keep ahead here. Turn right on to the lane and continue past the school (Hen Ysgol) and manor house to reach a T-junction. Turn right and continue to a footpath on the right.

4. This is signposted 'Calch Ty-Mawr'. Follow the track down towards the farm and bear left, over a stile next to a gate, immediately before the buildings. Continue along the hedge and turn right through a gate. Head down the left-hand edge of the field, passing through two gates, on either side of a track, and carry on in the same direction. At the bottom of the field, you'll come to your outward route where you turn left, through a gate, and retrace your steps back to the lakeside.

Where to eat and drink
There's a seasonal café and bar at the Lakeside Caravan Park, near the start of the walk, but if you want to good food and drink, pop into the excellent Castle Inn in Llangors village, which is situated north of the lake on the B4560.

What to see
If you walk down to the edge of the lake, you'll see a small artificial island or crannog just offshore. There's long been a myth telling of a submerged village beneath the lake and some have even told of hearing a church bell ring beneath the water. While this may be far-fetched, the lakeside was certainly inhabited by Iron Age Celts, and a dugout canoe found in the lake is displayed in the County Museum in Brecon.

While you're there
At the Multi Activity Centre on the outskirts of the village, you can go skytrekking (think zip wires), horse-riding, BMXing, climbing or you can get muddy and wet tackling the dingle scramble.

IN THE CWM CYNWYN VALLEY

DISTANCE/TIME	7 miles (11.3km) / 4hrs
ASCENT/GRADIENT	2,100ft (640m) / ▲ ▲ ▲
PATHS	Well-defined paths and tracks, short distance on quiet lanes, several stiles
LANDSCAPE	Lofty peaks, angular ridges and magnificent valleys
SUGGESTED MAP	OS Explorer OL12 Brecon Beacons National Park
START/FINISH	Grid reference: SO025248
DOG FRIENDLINESS	Care needed near sheep, some steep cliffs
PARKING	Car park at end of small lane, 3 miles (4.8km) south of Brecon
PUBLIC TOILETS	None on route

Few stories are quite as much as the tragic tale of Tommy Jones. In August 1900, the five-year-old and his father were walking from the railway station in Brecon to his grandfather's farm in Cwm Llwch. They rested a while at the army camp at Login where Tommy's grandfather and his 13-year-old cousin, Willie, met them. The two men decided to stay a while with the soldiers but the two boys continued on to the farmhouse, 0.5 miles (800m) away. As darkness fell, Tommy got scared. Willie wanted to continue to the farmhouse, but Tommy decided to return to his father. Sadly, he never made it. Willie rejoined the men shortly and, realising that the boy had vanished, a huge search ensued. As the days went by, there were suggestions that he'd been kidnapped or murdered. Remarkably, a few weeks later, a local woman dreamed about the boy and, although she had never been there before, was able to lead her husband up on to the ridge where they discovered Tommy's remains. A simple stone obelisk was erected close to the spot where the body was found. It was moved slightly in 1997, as the area surrounding it had become badly eroded.

This is far and away the most spectacular route up on to the highest ground of the National Park. The jagged ridges, steep gullies and deeply gouged valleys pay more than a passing resemblance to those of the higher mountains of Snowdonia, many miles further north. It's only the popularity of the peaks, which are easily reached from the road, which prevents it from feeling like a really wild day out in the mountains. The biggest climb comes early on, with a steep pull up from the car park on to the head of the lovely and remote Cwm Gwdi. The path then follows rocky, disused quarry tracks before hurdling the grassy spur that leads on to Cefn Cwm Llwch. The ridge is by no means knife-edge, but it does feel incredibly airy, dividing two magnificent valleys, both cradling fast-flowing mountain streams. The rocky ramparts of the summit seem to taunt you as you continue southwards and then, as you reach the steep final step, the spectacular northeastern face of Pen y Fan presents itself in its full glory. This is probably the most magnificent section of mountain scenery in the whole National Park. Steep gullies drop down from the summit, vaulting vertical crags as they plummet into the valley below. The summit, often crowded, can come as an anti-climax after the wild scenery, but it's a great mountain and there's plenty more on the descent from Corn Du. After crossing the void between the peaks, you'll trace the airy tops of Craig Cwm Llwch past the Tommy Jones obelisk, one of the Beacons' best-known landmarks. You'll then drop to a fine example of a glacial lake, Llyn Cwm Llwch, which makes an excellent picnic spot, surrounded still by the formidable walls of the head of the valley.

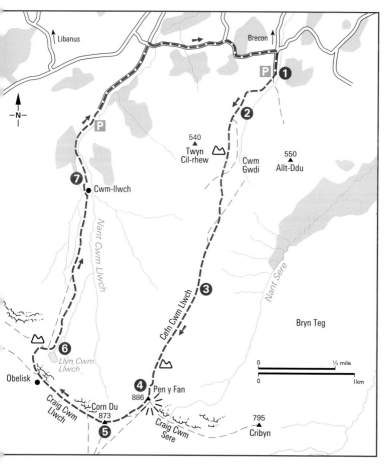

1. Walk uphill from the car park and pass an information plinth before crossing a stile. Walk along the right-hand side of the field towards the top right-hand corner and then bear left to continue along the fence to reach another stile.

2. Follow the broad but faint grassy track straight on. As it reaches steeper ground, it becomes a better-defined stony track that swings slightly left and climbs the hillside. Continue ahead, up towards the head of Cwm Gwdi, and keep ahead, ignoring a few right forks, until the path eventually levels out on Cefn Cwm Llwch.

3. Continue along the ridge towards the summit ahead. As you reach the foot of the peak, the track steepens considerably, offering a fine viewpoint over a perilous gully that drops into Cwm Sere on the left. Continue to climb steeply over a few rocky steps to reach the summit cairn on Pen y Fan.

4. Bear right to follow the escarpment edge and drop into a shallow saddle beneath the rising crest of Corn Du. Fork right up on to this summit, then bear left for a few paces to locate a steep path that drops down through rocky outcrops on to easier ground below. Bear right and drop past the summit.

5. Continue down the hill forking right to pass the Tommy Jones obelisk with the steep crags of Craig Cwm Llwch on your right-hand side. Above the lake, the path forks; take the right-hand option and right again at the next fork to drop steeply, around a dog-leg and over moraine banks to the lake shore.

6. A clear track leads north from the lake, alongside the outflow; follow it over easy ground to cross a stile that leads on to a broad farm track. Take this down to a gate in front of a building and climb the stile on the left. Cross the compound and climb another stile to follow waymarker posts around to the right on to another track, beyond the building.

7. Bear left on to this track and follow it down, over a footbridge, to a parking area. Keep straight ahead, through a gate to a crossroads, where you turn right. Cross the bridge and continue for over a mile (1.6km) ignoring turning to left to another T-junction. Turn right and walk uphill back to the car park.

Where to eat and drink

There's nothing close to the walk, but Brecon, 3 miles (4.8km) to the north, has plenty of choice including pubs, bars, coffee shops and cafés. Alternatively, for a cuppa and a cake, try the National Park Visitor Centre near Libanus.

What to see

As you descend from the escarpment into Cwm Llwch, you'll drop to the shores of Llyn Cwm Llwch, a fine example of a mountain lake left behind by the last ice age. As the glaciers that shaped the head of the valley retreated, the rocks and stones that they had scoured from the steep slopes were deposited at their feet creating a wall, or bank, known as moraine. This effectively creates a dam for the lake to form.

While you're there

Merthyr Tydfil is one of South Wales' most fascinating towns – even its name, which was derived from the story of Tydfil, a martyred Welsh princess, is full of intrigue. The town's hey-day came during the Industrial Revolution when it was the most populated town in Wales. It now boasts a great museum in the shape of Cyfartha Castle, which sheds light on a chequered and often bloody past.

CRAIG CERRIG-GLEISIAD NATURE RESERVE

DISTANCE/TIME	4 miles (6.4km) / 2hrs
ASCENT/GRADIENT	1,050ft (320m) / ▲ ▲
PATHS	Clear footpaths and broad stony tracks
LANDSCAPE	Imposing crags and rolling moorland, great views
SUGGESTED MAP	OS Explorer OL12 Brecon Beacons National Park
START/FINISH	Grid reference: SN972221
DOG FRIENDLINESS	Take care near livestock, on lead in nature reserve
PARKING	Pull-in by small picnic area on A470, 2 miles (3.2km) north of Storey Arms
PUBLIC TOILETS	None on route

This is a short walk but it has much to offer. Firstly, there are some fine views over the Tarell Valley to the true kings of the National Park, Pen y Fan and Corn Du, whose lofty crowns command your attention for most of the way round. And secondly, the daunting crags of Craig Cerrig-gleisiad are a true spectacle in their own right and are well worth admiring close up, both from below and above.

This is a unique environment and, as such, it hosts a range of habitats that support a number of rare species of flora and fauna. The cirque (bowl-shaped basin) itself was formed by the action of an ice-age glacier, which scoured out a deep hollow in the hillside and then deposited the rocks it had accumulated at the foot of the cliff to form banks of moraine. The retreating ice left a legacy – a selection of arctic-alpine plants that were sheltered from the rising temperatures by the north-facing escarpment. These plants, which include saxifrages and roseroot, also need a lime-rich soil, present on the escarpments but not on the more acidic moorland on the tops.

The cliffs only make up a fraction of the 156-acre (63ha) National Nature Reserve. One of the things that makes Craig Cerrig-gleisiad – which means 'Blue-stone Rock' – special is the diversity of the terrain. The lower slopes are home to mixed woodland and flowers such as orchids and anemones, while the high ground supports heather and bilberry. You'll see plenty of sheep within the reserve, but grazing is controlled to ensure a variety of habitats. The diversity isn't just restricted to plants either – 16 species of butterfly have been recorded on the reserve and over 80 different types of birds, including the ring ouzel, or mountain blackbird as it's often known, and the peregrine falcon, which is definitely a bird of the cliffs. This mainly upland region of the Bannau Brycheiniog (Brecon Beacons) National Park is partitioned from the central Brecon Beacons by the deep slash of the Taf and Tarell valleys. The name Fforest Fawr, which means Great Forest, comes not from trees but from its one-time status as a royal hunting ground. The high ground is largely untracked and barren, but the north-facing escarpment, of which Craig Cerrig-gleisiad forms a part, is steep and impressive. As the land dips to the south, it is chiselled into a succession of north–south running valleys that cradle the infant forms of some of the National Park's greatest rivers. These are seen to best effect on the southern fringes of the park, where they form Fforest Fawr's greatest spectacle, Waterfall Country.

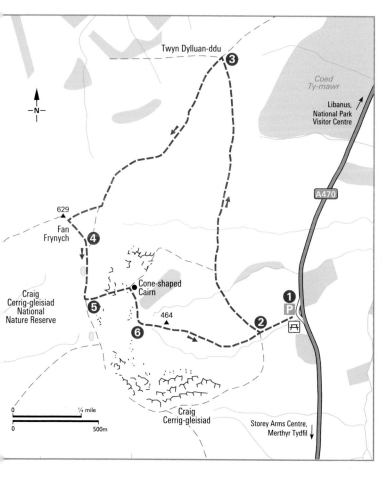

1. There's a bridge and a small picnic area at the southern end of the lay-by. Go through the kissing gate on the other side of the bridge to the picnic area. Head towards the crags, following a clear footpath, until you come to a gap in the next wall.

2. Pass through this and turn right to follow a dry-stone wall north. Head down into a small valley and cross the stream to continue in the same direction. Drop into another, steeper, valley and climb out, still following the track. Continue through the bracken to a kissing gate.

3. Cross and turn left on to a stony track. Follow this up to a gate and a stile and continue through rough ground, churned up by mining, until it levels on a dished plateau. Bear right here to the whitewashed trig point of Fan Frynych, then turn sharp left to return to the main track above the escarpment.

4. Turn right on to the main track again and continue past more rough ground before dropping slightly into a broad but shallow valley. Near the bottom, go through a kissing gate on the left (signed 'Beacons Way').

5. Follow the obvious path straight ahead and cross the top of the steep hillside to a beautifully built cone-shaped cairn. Turn right here to drop steeply all the way down into the heart of the nature reserve, following regular waymarker posts.

6. As the ground levels, bear around to the right to follow a signed diversion and continue alongside the stream to the gap in the wall you passed through earlier. Go through again and follow the outward path back to the car park.

Where to eat and drink

The National Park Visitor Centre, 2 miles (3.2km) west of Libanus, serves tasty breakfasts, lunches and snacks, as well as delicious cakes. If you fancy a pub, there's the Tai'r Bull Inn, in Libanus.

What to see

Much of the outward leg follows the line of a pristine dry-stone wall. Although changes in farming practices in the hills haven't altered as radically as they have in many lowland areas, the hedgerows and walls that once divided the land are expensive to maintain and have been slowly replaced by wire fences. The National Park Authority provides free consultation to landowners wishing to keep the more scenic traditional crafts alive.

While you're there

This is the nearest walk to the National Park Visitor Centre on Mynydd Illtud Common, near Libanus. It's a great source of information about the National Park, hosts some great displays and has a programme of guided walks.

INTO FFOREST FAWR

DISTANCE/TIME	7.25 miles (11.8km) / 3hrs 30min
ASCENT/GRADIENT	1,750ft (530m) / ▲ ▲ ▲
PATHS	Some clear paths/tracks, but also sketchy moorland paths across boggy terrain (6 stiles)
LANDSCAPE	Imposing crags and rolling moorland, great views
SUGGESTED MAP	OS Explorer OL12 Brecon Beacons National Park
START/FINISH	Grid reference: SN982202
DOG FRIENDLINESS	Take care near livestock, on lead in nature reserve
PARKING	Pull-in by small picnic area on A470, 2 miles (3.2km) north of Storey Arms Centre
PUBLIC TOILETS	None on route
NOTES	Difficult navigation in poor visibility

The untracked moorland of Fforest Fawr sees far fewer visitors than the mountains on the other side of the main thoroughfare. Admittedly, the rounded peaks of Fforest Fawr lack the majesty and distinction of the undisputed kings of the national park, Pen y Fan and Corn Du. They will nevertheless appeal to those who enjoy the solitude of wild, open moorland, and for this reason, it is always refreshing to escape the crowds and climb the highest and most accessible mountain in the range, Fan Fawr.

The most direct approach to the summit starts from opposite the Storey Arms Centre. This walk begins further north, however, from Craig Cerrig-gleisiad, and begins with a dramatic ascent. From the top, the bulky summit of Fan Fawr can be clearly seen to the south, and the wild moorland crossing to its lower slopes provides a good introduction to the type of walking found in this area.

After the peace and solitude of Fan Fawr, the crowds and busyness surrounding the Storey Arms Centre can come as a shock. Now an outdoor activities centre, it was originally built as a coaching inn on the high point of the mountain road between Merthyr Tydfil and Brecon. Tired horses at the top of the climb would be replaced with fresh teams from the inn's stables, while travellers and drivers would be offered refreshments. North of the Storey Arms Centre, the old coaching road runs along the opposite side of the Tarell Valley to the A470. It remains a pleasant metalled track and provides a good example of how roads were once built. A layer of small, broken stones was laid down, each less than an inch in diameter. The wooden coach wheels passing over these would grind dust into the gaps between them, thereby creating a solid track.

Running below the level of the road is the Afon Tarell, a beautiful stream that descends through a glaciated valley to the River Usk near Brecon. Much of the land either side of the river is owned by the National Trust, and there are a number of permissive paths for visitors to explore the valley. The upper reaches of the river are home to otters and dippers, while salmon and sewin (sea trout) are occasional migratory visitors.

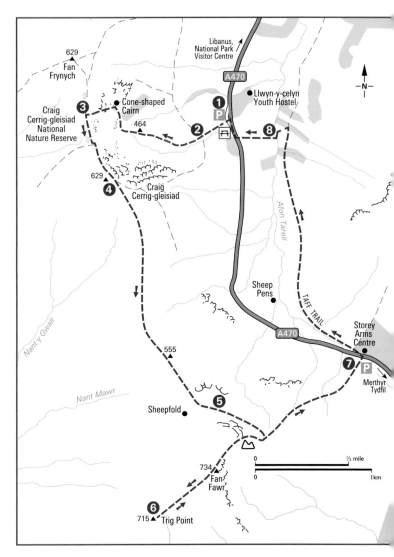

1. From the lay-by, go through a kissing gate on to a gravel path (this is on the other side of the stream from the picnic area). Pass an information board and climb through trees to a wooden gate in a dry-stone wall. Directly ahead are the towering crags of Craig Cerrig-gleisiad.

2. Go through a gap in the wall and take the path climbing straight ahead. As the ground levels, bear left to follow a signed diversion. Following regular

waymark posts, climb steeply to the right until you reach a junction of paths at a cone-shaped cairn. Turn sharply left and continue more easily to a kissing gate in a fence.

3. Go through the gate and turn left on to a stony track, which follows a fence along the top of Craig Cerrig-gleisiad's high cliffs. Drop to a stile and gate by a pond and continue straight up the hill ahead, still following a boundary fence and wall. A pile of stones marks the summit of Craig Cerrig-gleisiad.

4. Where the wall on your left drops away down the slope, keep ahead towards Fan Fawr, following a faint path across the wide, open moor. After negotiating a boggy plateau, the path climbs for a short distance before cutting left, across the steep slope, to pick up a narrow ledge path around the mountain's north-eastern flank.

5. Maintaining height, continue around the mountain until an obvious grassy path is met (this is the main track ascending from the Storey Arms Centre). Turn right and climb steeply to a cairn marking the summit of Fan Fawr. Continue to a trig point about 720yds (660m) southwest of the summit.

6. Return down the steep slope climbed earlier and continue downhill in the direction of the Storey Arms Centre. Keep straight ahead across a flatter marshy area, using the clearly visible path to Pen y Fan as a distant landmark. Once over a small rise, drop to a car park on the A470 opposite the Storey Arms Centre.

7. Cross the busy main road and bear left on to a track signed 'Taff Trail'. Descend steadily, separated from the A470 by the deepening valley of the Tarell river. At a sign for Llwyn-y-celyn Youth Hostel, turn left over a stile and drop down to a footbridge across the Afon Tarell.

8. Ignore the signed path right to the youth hostel and keep straight ahead up a steep field towards two trees on the brow of the hill. Continue past the trees to a stile at the top of the field and turn right along the A470. Cross the road carefully to return to your starting point.

Where to eat and drink
The National Park Visitor Centre, 2 miles (3.2km) west of Libanus, serves tasty breakfasts, lunches and snacks, as well as delicious cakes. If you fancy a pub, there's the Tai'r Bull Inn, in Libanus. This serves good pub food, has a cozy bar and a roaring log fire.

What to see
Sheep grazing has been an important economic activity on Fforest Fawr for centuries. Look out for a circular stone sheepfold just north of Fan Fawr, and also a number of stone-built sheep pens next to the Afon Tarell. Sheep would be collected in these pens to be washed before being taken to market.

While you're there
Along with Walk 33, this is the nearest walk to the National Park Visitor Centre on Mynydd Illtud Common, near Libanus. It's a good source of information about the Bannau Brycheiniog (Brecon Beacons) National Park, hosts some great displays and has a programme of guided walks.

THE PEN Y FAN PILGRIMAGE

DISTANCE/TIME	5 miles (8km) / 2hrs 30min
ASCENT/GRADIENT	1,610ft (491m) / ▲ ▲
PATHS	Clearly defined tracks
LANDSCAPE	Rugged high mountains and deeply scooped valleys
SUGGESTED MAP	OS Explorer OL12 Brecon Beacons National Park
START/FINISH	Grid reference: SN982203
DOG FRIENDLINESS	Care needed near sheep and on cliff tops
PARKING	Lay-by on A470, opposite the Storey Arms Centre
PUBLIC TOILETS	At Pont ar Daf car park

Every mountain has its 'trade route' – the easiest and most trafficked way to the top – and Pen y Fan is no different. At 2,907ft (886m), this is the highest peak in southern Britain and the closest real mountain to a vast chunk of the population, attracting huge visitor numbers. The most commonly used tactic is an out-and-back approach, using the motorway-like track that heads west from the southern edge of the small plantation, but this is less rewarding than the simple circular route described here, which starts by crossing the head of the Taff Valley.

The geology of Pen y Fan includes a fascinating hotchpotch of rocks. Pen y Fan is composed of old red sandstone laid down during the Devonian period. However, this is not just one uniform stone but different stones from three separate formations. The lower sections are sandstone and mudstone from the Senni Beds Formation, the stones towards the top are from the Brownstones Formation, whilst the summit (and that of nearby Corn Du) are sandstones from the Plateau Beds Formation.

Right next door to Pen y Fan, and easily accessible from it across a short saddle, is Corn Du (from the Welsh for 'black horn' and pronounced corn dee). Just 43ft (13m) lower than its illustrious neighbour, it's the home of a Bronze Age burial cairn. Below it, to the northwest, is Cwm Llwch, a glacial lake, while just along the ridge towards Pen Milan is the obelisk on which is told the sad story of five-year-old Tommy Jones (see walk 32).

Over the years, Pen y Fan and the surrounding mountains have claimed a number of lives due to sudden bad weather moving in. Do check the forecast beforehand and if the conditions aren't favourable, don't go. On bright sunny days, a trip up Pen y Fan is an unforgettable experience – on the very clearest you can see from Preseli Hills to the Black Mountains and as far south as Exmoor. However, when the weather closes in, visibility can drop to almost nothing very quickly, so the risk you've taken heading up will be for nothing.

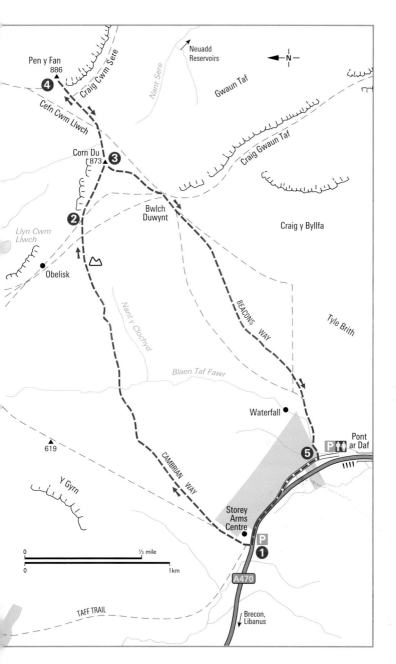

1. Cross the road and go through the gate next to the telephone box. The large building to your right is the Storey Arms, now an outdoor education centre but once a wayside inn on the coaching road between Brecon and South Wales. The original road can be seen forking off to your left, forming a section of the Taff Trail, a long distance route between Cardiff and Brecon. Follow a clear path up the hillside, leaving the plantation behind and crossing the open

moorland of the southern flanks of Y Gyrn – a rounded summit to your left. You'll soon gain the ridge and go through a kissing gate to drop easily down to the infant Taf Fawr – a pleasant and sheltered spot, ideal for a break before you reach the exposed hilltops above. The way ahead is clear, with a man-made track climbing steeply up the hillside opposite. Follow this, keeping straight ahead at a fork near the top, until it reaches the escarpment edge above the magnificent valley of Cwm Llwch. Below you'll see the glacier-formed lake of Llyn Cwm Llwch, and above this the steep head wall that unites the twin peaks.

2. Turn right to follow the clear path up towards the rocky ramparts of Corn Du. The path slips easily around the craggy outcrops and leads you up to the huge cairn on top of the broad summit plateau. The views down the valley are awesome, but take care as some of the summit rocks pretty much overhang the chasm below.

3. The way to Pen y Fan is obvious from here. Drop into the shallow saddle to the east and continue easily on to the summit. This opens up a whole new vista, with the narrow ridge of Cefn Cwm Llwch acting as the dividing wall for the remote Cwm Sere, to the right as you look out.

4. The northeast face of the mountain is particularly precipitous so take care near the edges. The most enjoyable way to begin your descent is to retrace your steps across Corn Du (Point 3) and turn left to Bwlch Duwynt, the obvious saddle between the summit and the long ridge that runs south. Alternatively, a good path runs below Corn Du, allowing easy passage with no extra height gain. To locate this, drop back into the saddle you've just crossed and fork left, beneath the grassy slope that leads to the summit. The views from this section are to the south, over the two currently drained, Neuadd reservoirs. Bwlch Duwynt represents a fairly major junction of paths, but you'll easily locate the main track that forks downhill to your right, away from Corn Du. Again, sections of this track have been laid in stone to slow the erosion caused by thousands of walkers' feet. Follow the track easily down for just over a mile (1.6km) until you see the Taf Fawr river to your right-hand side. A short diversion to your right near the bottom will reveal a great, rocky picnic spot, situated above a small waterfall. Cross the bridge over the river and go through the kissing gate into the main car park.

5. Turn right into the car park and follow it to its end where a broad dirt track takes over. Continue along the side of the plantation and cross the road to return to the start.

Where to eat and drink
The Tai'r Bull Inn at Libanus, on the A470, southwest of Brecon, is a fine pub with a wood burning stove and a cosy inglenook fireplace. The selection of food is diverse and they also serve a good pint. Alternatively, try the National Park Visitor Centre also near Libanus, which has a great coffee shop.

ABOVE THE CAERFANELL VALLEY

DISTANCE/TIME	5.5 miles (8.8km) / 3hrs 30min
ASCENT/GRADIENT	1,542ft (470m) / ▲ ▲ ▲
PATHS	Clear tracks across open mountain tops, along river and through forest, some mud and wet peat
LANDSCAPE	Moorland, craggy escarpments, remote valley, coniferous plantation, waterfalls
SUGGESTED MAP	OS Explorer OL12 Brecon Beacons National Park
START/FINISH	Grid reference: SO056175
DOG FRIENDLINESS	Care needed near livestock
PARKING	Large car park, 3 miles (4.8km) west of Talybont Reservoir
PUBLIC TOILETS	None on route

In only 5.5 miles (8.8km), this walk encapsulates almost every sort of landscape found in the National Park. It starts by climbing steeply on to an impressive peak from where you track easily along a steep sandstone escarpment, so typical of the area's high mountain scenery. The airy path crosses the head of a precipitous waterfall, rubs shoulders with an expansive moorland plateau and provides views that will remain in your memory for a long time. At the half-way stage, you'll get a sneak peep of the highest peaks in the National Park as well as a bird's-eye view over Cwm Oergwm, one of the most spectacular valleys in a wild land that's famed for them. The return leg passes the forlorn wreckage of a Canadian warplane and a fitting memorial to those who perished in her, before dropping easily down to follow a delightful upland river past a series of tumbling waterfalls. It finishes with a steep pull up through a small plantation, with further cascades and rapids.

As you approach the clearly visible cairn beneath Waun Rydd, a sharp eye will spot flashes of red, draped over the impeccable stonework. As you draw closer, you'll see that the red is in fact, a plethora of poppy wreaths hung over a simple memorial. A bronze plaque lists the names of the young Canadians who lost their lives when Wellington bomber R1645 came down in bad weather, following a routine training flight on 6 July, 1942. The twisted wreckage, a deathly shade of dull grey, lies strewn around the bracken-covered hillside below the cairn. The serenity and beauty of the Beacons' landscape makes a fitting backdrop to the scene and it's always difficult to pass this spot without pausing for reflection.

Gigfran is Welsh for raven and the diminutive crag that shades the memorial is named after these powerful birds that can often be seen performing aerobatics above it. They are the largest members of the corvid family, easily distinguished from carrion crows, rooks, jackdaws and the rarer chough, by their size. Ravens are synonymous with remote upland areas and rugged coastal regions, where they tend to nest on crags and perform tumbling flight displays that appear more for pleasure than for purpose. Although the majority of their nourishment in the mountain environment comes from sheep carrion, they are endlessly resourceful and incredibly skillful hunters too.

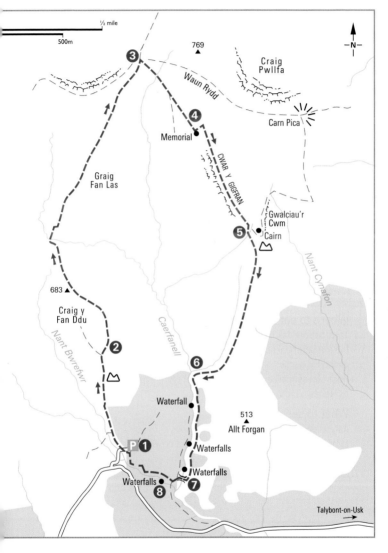

1. Walk back out of the car park, either crossing the cattle grid or a kissing gate to the left of it, then turn immediately right on to a stone track that heads uphill, with the stream on your left. Follow this track steeply up to the top of the escarpment and keep straight ahead to cross the narrow spur, where you bear around, slightly to the left, to follow the escarpment.

2. Stay on the clear path, with the escarpment to your right, for about 1.5 miles (2.4km), till you meet a number of paths at the head of the valley.

3. Take the sharp right turn to follow a narrow track slightly downwards, around the head of the valley, towards the cliffs that can be seen on the opposite hillside. Keep left at a fork and continue to the crash memorial.

4. Almost directly above the memorial, you'll see a rocky gully leading up on to the ridge. On the left-hand side of this, as you look at it, is a faint track that climbs steeply up. Take this to the top and turn right on to a narrow but clear track. Follow this track easily above the crag, to a distinctive cairn at the southern end of the ridge. Just north of the cairn you'll see a small stream.

5. Follow this down for 30ft (9m) to join a clear grassy track that trends leftwards at first, then follows a clear groove down the spur. This becomes an easy footpath that crosses a broad plateau and a bog and then leads to a junction at a wall. Turn right here and drop down to the Afon Caerfanell.

6. Cross the stile on your left at the bottom and follow the narrow footpath down-stream, past a number of waterfalls. Eventually you'll pass the largest of them and come to a footbridge.

7. Cross the footbridge and go through a kissing gate to follow the track into the forest. Pass some ruined buildings on your right, and before you cross the small bridge, turn right on to a clear path that leads uphill into the forest with waterfalls on your left.

8. Continue uphill on the main track, crossing a stream and taking optional detours to the left and right to see other waterfalls. Eventually you'll meet a broader forest track where you turn left and climb up to a gravel path where you turn left up to the car park.

Where to eat and drink

Talybont-on-Usk has several pubs, including the Traveller's Rest, 500yds (457m) southeast of the village on the road to Llangynidr, which has a canalside garden and a good restaurant. There's also the Old Barn Tea Room (seasonal) a little over a mile (1.6km) south of the start on the road to Merthyr Tydfil.

What to see

As you progress along the grassy slopes of the uplands, you'll become familiar with the sight of small, mottled brown birds that flee upon your approach. These are either skylarks or meadow pipits and although they look similar at first sighting, they can easily be told apart. The skylark is slightly larger, lighter in colour, has a stouter beak and a small crest on its head. The pipit makes a dipping flight, while the skylark is well known for its continuous song, usually performed as it hovers high above you.

THE TAF FECHAN VALLEY

DISTANCE/TIME	9 miles (14.5km) / 4hrs 30 min
ASCENT/GRADIENT	2,395ft (730m) / ▲ ▲ ▲
PATHS	Clear well-trodden paths, boggy patches, broad rocky track
LANDSCAPE	Steep rocky escarpments overlooking deep U-shaped valley
SUGGESTED MAP	OS Explorer OL12 Brecon Beacons National Park
START/FINISH	Grid reference: SO038169
DOG FRIENDLINESS	Care needed near livestock, several steep drops
PARKING	Neuadd car park towards end of lane heading north from Pontsticill
PUBLIC TOILETS	None on route

This is a fine way to visit the area's highest ground, particularly if you feel like a long outing but are afraid of over-committing yourself, as any, or all, of the big peaks can be by-passed if required. It's also an easy way to gain the tops, as it starts at an altitude over 1,300ft (396m) and, with the exception of two short but stiff sections, the climbing remains gentle to the point of being almost undetectable.

The Taf Fechan has certainly carved itself a beautiful valley. Its grand sweeping architecture doesn't appear any the worse for the addition of the Neuadd reservoirs. Built to supply water to Merthyr Tydfil during the Industrial Revolution, in recent years the dam walls have shown their age and a decision was taken to drain both reservoirs. Subsequently, the lower reservoir dam wall has been totally removed. The upper reservoir will remain drained until it is required once again.

Once up, the walk cruises easily along the sandstone promenade of Graig Fan Ddu and Craig Gwaun Taf, offering great views across the magnificent cwm to the steep head of the valley, where the two highest peaks in southern Britain preside. It also rewards the walker with some tantalising glimpses of the stunning and seldom visited valley of Cwm Crew, which runs southwest from the narrowest section of the ridge at Rhiw yr Ysgyfarnog – the Slope of the Hare.

The high peaks need little introduction. Their might and stature are clear from almost any viewpoint, although you may find yourself surprised by the sheer scale of the drop from the north face of Corn Du and the incomparable northeast face of Pen y Fan, which falls precipitously down over 1,000ft (305m) to the rolling moorland of Cwm Sere below. Not so surprising are the views from the top, which are magnificent and matched only by the elation of reaching the summit. As you'd expect, the highest peaks also act as a divide for the watersheds, with the water to the north draining into the Usk and the hills to the south feeding the Taff, which runs south to Cardiff.

Steep and rocky ground leads down from the table-top summit, with the grassy flanks of Cribyn appearing much steeper than they really are up ahead. If you don't think you can manage another climb, sneak around the peak to the right, otherwise, more fine views await you on the cramped summit. This time you can gaze north over Cwm Cynwyn, as fine a natural amphitheatre as you're ever likely to see. With the peaks bagged, you'll drop into the atmospheric rocky saddle of Bwlch ar y Fan and pick up an ancient track, known locally as the 'Gap Road'. Although many claim it is of Roman origin, the exact age of the track isn't known. It does, however, afford easy progress for tired legs back down to the valley floor. The grassy shores of the former lower lake make a great sun-trap and an excellent picnic spot from where you can look back up the valley to the impressive outlines of the mountains you've just climbed.

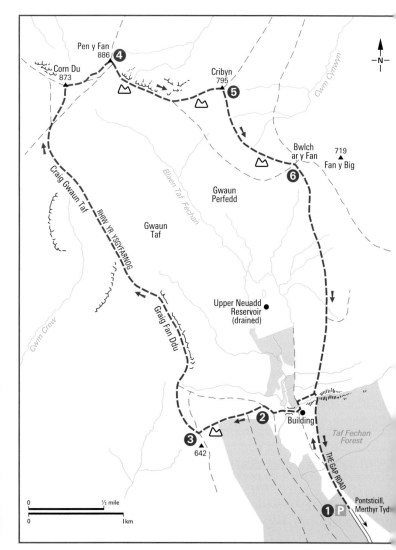

1. Leave the car park by the far end and head along the road to a gate. Just before it, take a stony track that bears off to the right. Pass through a gate and over a stream in a gully before turning left at a fork to go downhill to another gate. Go through this and turn left to yet another gate. Don't go through this but turn right down a path next to it. Cross the road at the bottom, turn right and, after a few paces, turn left down a path immediately after a Neuadd Reservoir sign. This path bends down to the right of a derelict building to a small footbridge. Climb up on to the bank opposite and bear left to walk along its top. This will take you to a gate that leads out on to open moorland.

2. Go through this and keep straight ahead, taking the left-hand of the two tracks, which leads uphill towards the edge of a mainly felled forest. Follow the clear track up, with the forest to your left, and then climb steeply up a stony gully to the top of the escarpment.

3. Once there, turn right on to the obvious path and follow the escarpment along for over 2.5 miles (4km). You'll eventually drop into a distinct saddle with the flat-topped summit of Corn Du directly ahead. Where the path comes to a crossroads, keep straight ahead and climb easily up on to the summit. Follow the escarpment edge along and then drop down into another saddle, where you take the path up on to the next peak, Pen y Fan.

4. Again, from the summit cairn, follow the escarpment around and drop steeply, on a rocky path, down into a deep col beneath Cribyn. Keep straight ahead to climb steeply up to the cairn on the narrow summit. Note: this climb can be avoided by forking right and following another clear path that contours right around the southern flanks of the mountain and brings you out at Point 6.

5. From the top, bear right and follow the escarpment around to the southeast. After a long flat stretch, you'll drop steeply down into to a deep col known as Bwlch ar y Fan.

6. Turn right on to the wellmade track that leads easily down the mountain. Follow this for over 1.5 miles (2.4km), until it forks. Turn left down to a stream and retrace your steps to the start.

Where to eat and drink
The most popular pubs in the area are at nearby Talybont-on-Usk (follow the narrow lane past the beautiful Talybont Reservoir), where the pick of the bunch is the Traveller's Rest, on the outskirts of the village towards Llangynidr. This has a delightful canal-side garden and a good restaurant.

What to see
The summits of Pen y Fan, Corn Du and Cribyn were once all crowned with Bronze Age burial cairns, probably dating back to around 1800 BC.

While you're there
Head south to Pant, north of Merthyr Tydfil, and take a ride aboard the Brecon Mountain Railway, a narrow-gauge steam train that takes a 90-minute return trip along the side of the Taf Fechan Reservoir to Torpantau (open from April to November).

WATERFALLS BELOW PORTH YR OGOF

DISTANCE/TIME	4 miles (6.4km) / 2hrs
ASCENT/GRADIENT	360ft (110m) / ▲ ▲ ▲
PATHS	Riverside paths and forest tracks, some rough sections and steps
LANDSCAPE	Wooded valleys, fast-flowing rivers, waterfalls
SUGGESTED MAP	OS Explorer OL12 Brecon Beacons National Park
START/FINISH	Grid reference: SN928124
DOG FRIENDLINESS	Rivers too powerful for fetching sticks and care needed near steep drops
PARKING	Car park at Porth yr Ogof, near Ystradfellte
PUBLIC TOILETS	In the car park
NOTES	The rocks above Sgwd yr Eira are unstable and it's recommended that you do not linger beneath the waterfall

In a National Park justly renowned for its sweeping, but barren, mountain scenery, lovers of high ground are in danger of completely overlooking one the park's hidden gems. This is the pocket of dramatic limestone scenery often referred to as Waterfall Country. South of the upland plateaux of Fforest Fawr, geological faults and water erosion have produced a series of deep, narrow gorges, sheltered by impressive woodland and randomly broken up by a succession of gushing waterfalls. The highlight of this is Sgwd yr Eira, where it's possible to venture right behind the falls. Walking here is a completely different experience to that of the windswept escarpments, but the scenery is marvellous and the generally sheltered nature of the terrain makes it an ideal outing for those days when cloud obscures the peaks.

In simple terms, the falls are the result of a geological fault that pushed the hard sandstone, which makes up the backbone of most of the National Park, up against softer shales. The force of the rivers, which spring up high on the mountains of Fforest Fawr, has eroded the shales leaving shelves of the harder rock exposed. These shelves are clearly visible on most of the falls.

At the southern edge of the high ground, a layer of carboniferous limestone overlies the old red sandstone. This younger rock is soluble in the slightly acidic rain and river water that constantly pounds it. The erosion results in caves like Porth yr Ogof at the start of this walk, where the rivers literally disappear underground, and craters where rainwater exploits weaknesses and faults in the rock – these are often referred to as sink holes or shake holes.

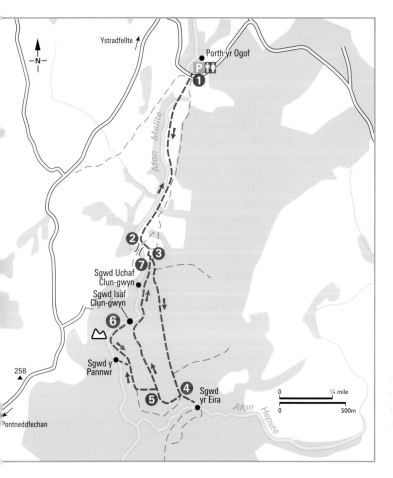

1. Cross the road at the entrance to the car park and head down the left-hand of the two paths, waymarked with a yellow arrow. Ignore a right fork marked 'Access for Cavers' and follow the main path through a kissing gate and on to the river bank. Now keep the river to your right to follow a rough footpath through a couple more kissing gates to reach a footbridge.

2. Don't cross but continue ahead on the main path to climb steeply up to a fence. Stay with the path, with a wooden fence now on your right, for a few paces and you'll reach a junction of footpaths marked with a large fingerpost. Bear sharp left on to a well-surfaced track, waymarked to Gwaun Hepste, and follow this for a short distance to another junction, where you should turn right (waymarked 'Sgwd yr Eira').

3. Continue walking along the well waymarked forest trail until another fingerpost directs you right, downhill. Follow this track to the edge of the forest and then bear around to the right. This track leads to the top of a set of wooden steps, on the left.

4. Go down the 167 steps to Sgwd yr Eira (Waterfall of the Snow) and then, having edged along the bank and walked behind the falls (waterproofs recommended), retrace your steps back up to the edge of the wood. Turn left and continue, still following the red-banded posts, to a fork marked with another fingerpost.

5. Turn left here (waymarked to Sgwd y Pannwr) and descend to the riverside. Turn left again to Sgwd y Pannwr (Fullers Falls), then turn around to walk upstream to Sgwd Isaf Clun-gwyn (Lower Waterfall of the White Meadow). Take care, the ground is very steep and rough around the best viewpoint.

6. Retrace your steps downstream to your original descent path and turn left to climb back up to the fork at the top (point 5). Turn left and follow the red-banded waymarkers along to Sqwd Uchaf Clun-gwyn. From here, continue along the main trail to the place where you split off earlier.

7. Drop back down to the footbridge and continue along the river bank to Porth yr Ogof.

Where to eat and drink
The New Inn in the small hamlet of Ystradfellte is about 1 mile (1.6km) from the start and incredibly popular with walkers, cyclists and cavers.

What to see
While the woods that line the river banks are home to many species of birds, the river itself is likely to offer sightings of the dipper. This bird is easy to spot, because it is dark brown and slightly smaller than a blackbird with a very visible white bib. It's usually seen bobbing up and down on rocks in mid-stream.

While you're there
Porth yr Ogof is accessed by following the steps down from the rear of the car park. You can walk in far enough to see the Pool of the White Horse, named after a strip of white calcite on the wall. Legend says it formed after a princess rode her horse into the cave while evading murderous pursuers. The horse fell and she drowned. Great care is needed around the cave entrance, as a fall could be fatal.

WATERFALLS AROUND PONTNEDDFECHAN

DISTANCE/TIME	7.75 miles (12.5km) / 3hrs 30min
ASCENT/GRADIENT	1,540ft (470m) / ▲ ▲
PATHS	Riverside paths and forest tracks, some rough sections and steps (6 stiles)
LANDSCAPE	Wooded valleys, fast-flowing rivers, waterfalls
SUGGESTED MAP	OS Explorer OL12 Brecon Beacons National Park
START/FINISH	Grid reference: SN911079
DOG FRIENDLINESS	Rivers too powerful for fetching sticks and care needed near steep drops
PARKING	The Craig y Ddinas forestry car park, northeast of Pontneddfechan
PUBLIC TOILETS	Opposite The Angel pub in Pontneddfechan
NOTES	The rocks above Sgwd yr Eira are unstable and it's recommended that you do not linger beneath the waterfall

During the 19th century, the southern edge of Waterfall Country was an important silica-mining area. Silica rock or quartzite was mined on a small scale in the Pontneddfechan area from the late 18th century, but the first large-scale mining operation began in 1822, when the Quaker entrepreneur William Weston Young took out a 21-year lease on land near the village. Major passageways were opened along the lower course of the Nedd Fechan (the path on the west bank is a former tramway) and in the Sychryd gorge near Craig y Ddinas. Young wanted silica to make firebricks, which he had found he could produce from high-quality 'Dinas' silica. After extraction, the rock was crushed in the valley then transported by horse-drawn tram to Pont Walby. A factory here turned the silica into firebricks, which were exported to line furnaces, lime kilns and domestic fireplaces across the globe.

Another important local industry was gunpowder, which was made on the Mellte river, north of Craig y Ddinas. The site was chosen for its isolation in the event of an explosion, its plentiful supply of water for powering machinery, and its ample supplies of timber for making charcoal. To contain any explosion, banks of earth were constructed between buildings, the latter usually being whitewashed so that any accumulation of powder could be more easily spotted. Workers on the site wore special safety slippers made out of leather, while horses were shod with copper shoes to prevent sparks. The works continued to make gunpowder until 1931, when a change in the law forced its closure. Most of the buildings were demolished for safety reasons the following year. Craig y Ddinas was also quarried for limestone (the car park is actually inside the former quarry).

Sgwd Gwladus on the Afon Pyrddin is often regarded as the prettiest of the Neath Valley waterfalls. The name of the fall is associated in legend with

Gwladus, a daughter of King Brychan of Brycheiniog. According to the story, Gwladus fell in love with a man called Einion, who for political reasons she was unable to marry. After death, their spirits were both invested in waterfalls along the Pyrddin river, Gwladus' in Sgwd Gwladus and Einion's in a fall about half a mile further upstream, Sgwd Einion Gam. Kept apart during life, their souls now merge in the pool below Sgwd Gwladus.

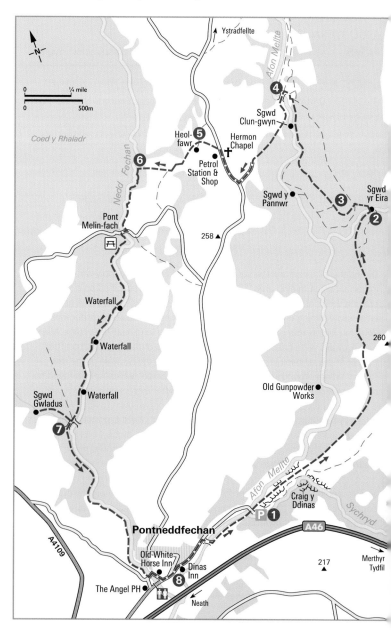

1. From the car park entrance, take a steeply climbing track signed to Sgwd yr Eira. After an initial stony ascent, the path continues more easily. Keep left where a stonier path forks downhill to the right. At the next fork, bear slightly right ('Sgwd yr Eira') and follow a well-marked path to a signed junction by an information board.

2. Turn left and drop steeply along a gravel path to the waterfall. Pass behind the curtain of water and clamber across wet, slippery boulders. Climb steeply (numerous steps) to a junction with a wide gravel path. Turn left and follow a well-marked path along the top edge of the valley.

3. Ignore a signed path on the left to Sgwd y Pannwr and continue to Sgwd Clun-gwyn. Keep ahead here ('Cwm Porth'), and take the next waymarked path descending left to the river. Continue upstream to a footbridge on the left.

4. Cross the bridge and climb along a gravel path above Sgwd Clun-gwyn. Bear left at a gravel drive to emerge at a road. Turn right and follow the road past a petrol station and tiny shop to reach a stile on the left, opposite a chapel. Walk diagonally across a field and follow markers to a junction with a drive.

5. Turn left and keep ahead past a house (Heol-fawr) on to a rough track. Pass round right- and left-hand bends to reach a permissive path on the right ('Tir Gofal'). Bearing slightly right, walk down a field to a gate. Bear left in the next field, then keep ahead (dropping steeply) to a stile above the Nedd Fechan river.

6. Turn left on to a narrow path, which follows the river downstream to a road. Turn right to cross a bridge and then left into the Pont Melin-fach picnic area. Follow the riverside path past a number of falls and rapids to a wooden foot-bridge on your left. Ignore this and continue to another bridge directly ahead.

7. Do not cross the bridge, but turn right on to a signed path to Sgwd Gwladus. After viewing the fall, retrace your steps to cross the bridge and continue along a wide gravel path down to the road at Pontneddfechan. Turn left to pass the Old White Horse Inn and then left again, on to the main road.

8. Where the main road bears left towards Ystradfellte, keep ahead past the Dinas Inn. Follow the road up to a footbridge on the right. Cross this to a junction with an enclosed track and turn left. At the end of the track, drop left to reach the entrance to the Craig y Ddinas car park.

Where to eat and drink
There are two excellent pubs in Pontneddfechan, The Angel and the Old White Horse Inn, both of which serve good food and real ale.

What to see
The deep river gorges of the Waterfall Country contain one of the richest and most extensive areas of ancient semi-natural woodland in Wales. High humidity and low levels of pollution provide an ideal habitat for rare ferns, lichens, mosses and liverworts.

GLAMORGAN HERITAGE COAST AT OGMORE

DISTANCE/TIME	6 miles (9.7km) / 2hrs 30min
ASCENT/GRADIENT	460ft (140m) / ▲
PATHS	Easy-to-follow across farmland and coastline, many stiles
LANDSCAPE	Deciduous woodland, farmland, bracken-covered sand dunes and rocky coastline
SUGGESTED MAP	OS Explorer 151 Cardiff & Bridgend
START/FINISH	Grid reference: SS885731
DOG FRIENDLINESS	Some difficult stiles; no dogs allowed on beach at Dunraven in summer
PARKING	Large car park at Heritage Centre above Dunraven Beach
PUBLIC TOILETS	Heritage Centre, also in Ogmore-by-Sea

Most visitors to South Wales overlook the chunk of land that lies south of the M4 motorway between Cardiff and Swansea. Yet surprisingly, smack bang between the two cities and overshadowed by the huge industrial complexes of Port Talbot, there lies an unspoilt strip of coast.

Granted Heritage Coast status in 1972, the 14-mile (22.5km) stretch of Glamorgan coastline that runs between Ogmore and Gileston stands as defiant against progress as its cliffs do against the huge ebbs and flows of the Bristol Channel tides. Sandy beaches, often punctuated by weathered strips of rock that dip their toes in the ocean, break up an otherwise formidable barrier of limestone and shale cliffs that rise and dip gracefully above the water.

Dunraven Bay houses the Heritage Centre, which offers displays and information about the area. It also makes an appropriate starting point for a walk that gives at least a taster of this unique landscape. The early stages track inland, through woodland and farmland before heading coastwards, at the small village of St Bride's Major. From here, the path sneaks between dunes and drops to the Ogmore River. Following the estuary downstream through bracken that simply teems with wildlife, you'll meet the coast at Ogmore-by-Sea and pick up the coast path above one of many beaches here. With ocean views to your right and the dunes to your left, you'll now climb easily back up above Dunraven where, if you time it right, you'll witness the cliffs reflecting the pastel shades of sunset as you enjoy the final drop to the beach. It's a wonderful way to finish off an evening stroll.

The Glamorgan Heritage Coast was one of three pilot schemes set up in 1972 to protect the country's unique coastal landscapes and environments from destructive development. There are now 15 such areas in Wales, accounting for over a third of the total coastline. The aims of the scheme are fourfold: to maintain the ecological diversity, to provide public access and encourage recreational use, to protect the needs of the local population, including farmers and landowners, and to preserve the quality of the coastline. The Glamorgan Heritage Coast is managed by the Countryside Council for Wales that employs a professional ranger service to take care of the day-to-day running of the area.

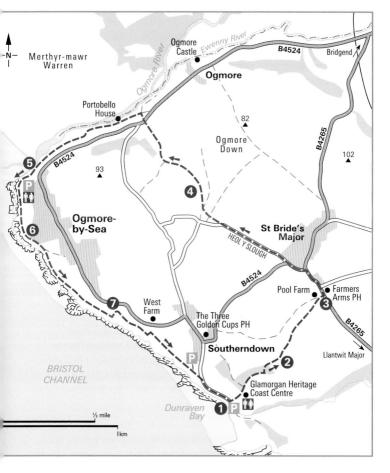

1. From the car park, head up the lane at the back of the car park and pass the Heritage Centre on the right. Keep walking straight ahead as the road swings left and go through a gate next to a stile to duck into woodland. Continue to a fork by a waymarker and a gap in the wall, where you keep left to reach a stile. Cross this stile and walk along the edge of the field to reach a stile on your left. Go over the stile, then cross a stone stile on your right to keep ahead with a hedge to your right.

2. Cross into another field and keep to the left-hand side, following the hedge-row, which is now on your left. When you reach the next stile, continue ahead, go past a gate on the left, to reach another stone stile on the left. Cross this stile and head right over another stile, next to a gate, to another stone stile between a house and the farmyard.

3. Turn left on to the road and walk into the village. Keep left into the Southerndown road then fork right into Heol-y-slough. Follow this road for 0.75 miles (1.2km) then, as the road bends left, continue across the common. Keep ahead where a bridleway crosses the track. As you join another track, maintain your direction along the valley floor.

4. The path winds its way down through sand dunes, passing a tributary valley on the left, and eventually emerges on the B4524. Cross the road and continue towards the river until you locate one of the many paths that lead left, parallel to the river, towards Portobello House. Keep left on the drive then, once above the house, continue along a clear path, again parallel to the Ogmore River.

5. Make sure you stay above the small cliffs as you approach the mouth of the estuary and you'll eventually arrive at a huge car parking area above the beach. Go through the car park along the coast around to the left.

6. You'll come to a stone wall, which will funnel you through a gate marked 'Coast Path'. Continue along the coast path until, 0.75 miles (1.2km) from the gate, you meet with a very steep-sided valley. Turn left into this valley then turn immediately right, on to a footpath that climbs steeply up the grassy hillside.

7. Stay with the footpath as it follows the line of a dry-stone wall around to West Farm. Keep the wall to the left to continue to the upper car park. A gap in the wall, at the side of this, leads you to a grassy track that follows the road down into Dunraven.

Where to eat and drink

Along the route you'll pass the Farmers Arms in St Bride's Major, which has a lounge bar and a separate eating area, serving Eastern Mediterranean style food. Another option is a short detour into Ogmore-by-Sea where there's plenty of choice of typical beach-side snacks such as chip shops and cafés. The Three Golden Cups at Southerdown is also worth the detour.

What to see

If the sea seems a long way out, it's worth remembering that the tidal flows in the Bristol Channel are the second largest in the world, with the differences between high and low water being well over 39ft (12m) on a high spring tide. The only tides larger than this are witnessed in Canada's Bay of Fundy.

While you're there

Only a mile (1.6km) from Ogmore-by-Sea is Ogmore Castle, a 12th-century Norman fortification that lies in a pretty green valley and is reputed to be the place where King Arthur was fatally wounded. His body is said to buried in a cave near by. True or not, the ruins are basic but atmospheric.

41

LLANTWIT MAJOR AND ST DONAT'S

DISTANCE/TIME	9 miles (14.5km) / 3hrs 30min
ASCENT/GRADIENT	790ft (240m) / ▲
PATHS	Coast path, well-marked field paths, tracks, minor roads and woodland trails (24 stiles)
LANDSCAPE	Coastal cliffs, fields, woodland, historic town
SUGGESTED MAP	OS Explorer 151 Cardiff & Bridgend
START/FINISH	Grid reference: SS967687
DOG FRIENDLINESS	Stone stiles may be difficult to negotiate
PARKING	Car park behind town hall in the centre of Llantwit Major (alternative parking available at railway station)
PUBLIC TOILETS	In town hall car park

There is no place more significant to the spread of early Christianity among the Celtic peoples than Llantwit Major. It was here, in the early 6th century, that St Illtyd re-established the famous divinity school of Cor Tewdws, which attracted pilgrims and pupils from throughout the Celtic world. More than 1,000 pupils attended the school at its height, including the future patron saints of Wales and Ireland, St David and St Patrick. The school was the axis around which the early Celtic church revolved, forging connections along the sea roads of the Atlantic with Cornwall, Brittany and Ireland.

Unfortunately, the original school and monastery were built of wood and have long since vanished. The present church is Norman in origin, but an interesting building in its own right. In 2013, a ruined chapel at the western end of the church (the Galilee) was fully restored and now houses a fabulous collection of Celtic stones and crosses formerly contained within the main church. A Latin inscription on the beautiful Houelt Cross refers to a Hywel ap Rhys, who was king of Glywysing (roughly, the old Glamorgan) in the late 9th century.

A mile or two to the west of Llantwit Major is the stunning St Donat's Castle. The original medieval fortress was founded by the Stradling family in the early 14th century; later on, during the 16th and 17th centuries, they enlarged and converted the castle into a great house, retaining original defensive features such as the battlemented curtain wall for ornamental effect.

After an amazing 23 generations, the Stradling connection with St Donat's came to an end. There were several changes of ownership before the site was bought in 1925 by the American newspaper magnate William Randolph Hearst. Hearst, a man of immense wealth and the inspiration behind Orson Welles' film *Citizen Kane* (1941), had seen photos of St Donat's in the magazine *Country Life*. Impressed, he spent a fortune renovating the castle in a style best described as Hollywood make-believe. According to George Bernard Shaw, St Donat's was 'what God would have built if he had had the money'. Under

Hearst's ownership, the castle was renowned for its celebrity parties, playing host to famous visitors such as Charlie Chaplin and a young John F. Kennedy. By the late 1930s, however, Hearst's newspaper empire had fallen on hard times, forcing him to put St Donat's on the market. Today, the building is home to a residential sixth-form college and a converted tithe barn in the grounds houses St Donat's Arts Centre.

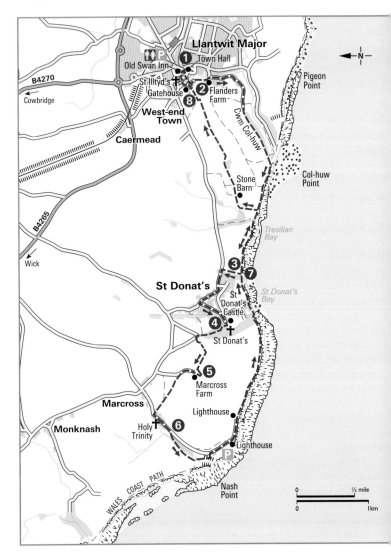

1. Turn right out of the car park, then left in front of the Old Swan Inn. Immediately bear left again, descending along Burial Lane to a stream crossing. Keep ahead up a flight of steps and turn left. Follow a track on to an enclosed path and continue to a stone stile on the right.

2. Cross into a field and follow the fence to the left. Drop through Flanders Farm to a lane and bear right. Follow a track along the top edge of Cwm

Col-huw to the coast and turn right. At Tresilian Bay, cross the stony beach, climbing steps to regain the coastal path.

3. After 0.5 miles (800m), take a path heading inland on the right. Turn left at a minor road and continue round a right-hand bend to reach a second set of gates on the left. Walk down the drive towards the castle and arts centre, then bear right on to a narrower lane signed to St Donat's Church.

4. Turn right before the church on to a woodland track and climb to a house. Keep ahead through the yard and take the lane forking left. Cross a stile on the left by a barn and follow waymarks to a field. Keep ahead, then cross a field on the right in the direction of Marcross Farm.

5. Meet a track in front of the farm and turn right. Keep ahead along a lane to a waymarked field gate on the left. Cross this and follow the hedge to the right. Climb a stone stile and follow the field edge ahead and then left. Continue into Marcross and turn left at a road.

6. Just after sewage works, pass through a gap on the right and drop to a stream. Cross over and bear left along a wooded valley. Turn left at the coast and climb to a car park. Follow the track past the lighthouses at Nash Point and join a clear coastal path to St Donat's Bay.

7. Rejoin your outward route. Just beyond Tresilian Bay, take a path on the left. Climb a high stone stile into fields and keep ahead past a stone barn. Maintain direction, crossing a stile signed to Llantwit Major. Aim left of a copse and then slightly left across a large field. Several stiles later, emerge on a track (Church Lane).

8. Keep ahead and join a tarmac lane to the Gatehouse. Drop left towards Illtyd's Church and follow the path through the graveyard. Climb past the town's central square to the Old Swan Inn. Turn right to return to the car park.

Where to eat and drink

There are plenty of places to eat and drink in Llantwit Major, but the Old Swan Inn in the centre of town is among the best of them. Elements of the pub building date back to the early 12th century, and there's a wonderfully cosy atmosphere inside. The pub offers an impressive selection of local guest ales and ciders, as well as an extensive food menu.

What to see

St Donat's is open on certain days of the year, usually for a festival or celebration like Christmas. Check their website for more details. The impressive cliffs along this part of the Glamorgan Heritage Coast consist typically of liassic limestones and shales. Prone to erosion, the cliffs are gradually retreating as they are undercut by winter storms.

While you're there

The historic centre of Llantwit Major – a delightful maze of tiny lanes, old stone buildings and atmospheric taverns – is well worth exploring further. Town guides are available from the tourist information centre inside the town hall.

42

CASTELL COCH AND THE TAFF TRAIL

DISTANCE/TIME	5.5 miles (8.8km) / 2hrs 30min
ASCENT/GRADIENT	920ft (280m) / ▲ ▲
PATHS	Forest tracks, disused railway line and clear paths, short section of tarmac
LANDSCAPE	Mixed woodland and open hillside with views over residential and industrial developments
SUGGESTED MAP	OS Explorer 151 Cardiff & Bridgend
START/FINISH	Grid reference: ST142839
DOG FRIENDLINESS	Care needed near livestock; not allowed in castle
PARKING	Fforest Fawr car park
PUBLIC TOILETS	None on route

A wooded hillside visible from the M4 motorway is hardly the place that you'd expect to find a fairy-tale castle, but at the bottom of the Taff Vale, just a few miles north of Cardiff, is one that easily rivals those of Bavaria. Castell Coch, with its red sandstone walls and conical towers, is worth a visit in its own right, but perched on a cliff top amid stunning deciduous woodland, it's also a great place to start a walk. Conveniently, two waymarked trails run close to the castle and these, together with a labyrinth of forest tracks, provide an invigorating circular route that shows some of the many different faces of the regenerated Valleys.

Every bit as captivating up close as it is from a distance, the majestic Castell Coch, now managed by CADW (Welsh Historic Monuments), was built in the late 1870s on the site of a 13th-century fortress. It had no military purpose whatsoever but was, in fact, a country retreat for the 3rd Marquess of Bute, who at the time was thought to be the richest man in the world and based his empire in Cardiff. Its design, by the architect William Burgess, who also designed St Finbar's Cathedral in Cork, is pure, unadulterated fantasy, with a working drawbridge and portcullis, three circular towers and a dream boudoir that features a lavishly decorated domed ceiling. The grandest of all the castle's rooms has to be the drawing room, three storeys high with a ribbed and vaulted ceiling, further decorated with birds and butterflies. The two-storey chimney piece boasts statues of the Three Fates, which show the thread of life being spun, measured and finally cut. Characters from Aesop's fables are also depicted.

The route away from the woods follows a section of the Taff Trail, a 55-mile (89km) waymarked route that leads from Cardiff Bay to Brecon via the Taff Valley, Llandaff, Pontypridd and Merthyr Tydfil. Most of the trail, including the lower section of this walk, is along disused railway lines, as well as forest tracks and canal paths. From the Taff Trail, this walk follows an airy section of the 21-mile (34km) Ridgeway Walk (Ffordd-y-Bryniau). It climbs steeply on to the narrow ridge of Craig yr Allt, which is a spectacular viewpoint.

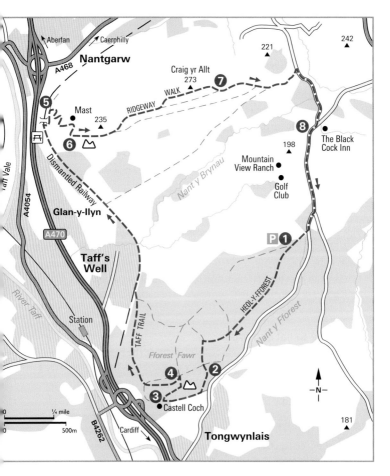

1. Start in the car park at the Forestry Commission sign, head deeper into the car park, and then turn left after 54yds (50m), on to a clear footpath marked by a 'no horse-riding' sign. Follow this path, ignoring tracks on both the right and left (two of which are flanked by blue posts), until the posts become blue on your path and you come to a T-junction by a sign forbidding horse-riding. Cross the small brook and turn left to continue steeply down hill, past a turning on the left.

2. The track eventually swings around to the right and descends to meet the drive for Castell Coch. Turn right up the drive towards the castle.

3. Walk up to the castle entrance and turn right to walk to a metal information board. Take the path next to this and climb steeply on a good path past a waymark post and through a gap in the fence to a junction of tracks.

4. Turn sharp left, signposted 'The Taff Trail', and follow this broad forest track around the hillside and then down, where it meets the disused railway line close to some houses. Pass through the barrier on the right and follow the clear track for over 1 mile (1.6km) until you pass a picnic area and come to another barrier.

5. Go through the barrier then, as you come to a disused bridge, turn right over a stile, signposted 'Glamorgan Ridgeway Walk'. Take this and follow it for about 76yds (70m) and then around to the right. Ignore one turn left and then turn sharp left to zig-zag back across the hillside, where you turn right again. Follow the main path as it zig-zags up the hillside, aiming at the mast and then, as you reach the field edge, bear right once more. This leads up to a post on a narrow ridge where you turn left.

6. Climb steeply up the ridge and continue, with high ground to your left, until you reach a clear path that leads left by a post, up to the ridge top. Follow this and bear right at the top to walk easily along, with great views. Keep ahead to drop slightly and then bear left on to a broad track that rises up and carries on along the ridge over Craig yr Allt.

7. Follow it down through the bracken ignoring the turn to right. Bear right onto the track down to a kissing gate that leads on to a tarmac drive. Turn left and continue past some houses on the right-hand side to a junction by The Black Cock Inn. Turn right and climb up to another junction, where you bear right.

8. Carry on past the golf club, then fork right on to a narrow lane that drops and bears around to the left. Turn right here back to the car park.

Where to eat and drink
For good pub food, stop on your way round at The Black Cock Inn or alternatively, head back there once you've finished. Castell Coch has a decent tea room if you're planning a visiting.

What to see
Fforest Fawr is a great place to spot woodland birds and mammals. Grey squirrels are common and they are often blamed for the demise of the smaller red squirrel in this country. However, recent research has shown that this is more likely due to habitat loss.

While you're there
Pay your respects by the graves of the 144 people killed by the collapse of a giant spoil heap in Aberfan in October 1966. The horrific landslide engulfed the Pantglas Primary School, burying 116 children.

TWMBARLWM AND CWMCARN

DISTANCE/TIME	3 miles (4.8km) / 1hr 30min
ASCENT/GRADIENT	1,017ft (310m) / ▲ ▲
PATHS	Clear footpaths and forest tracks
LANDSCAPE	Steep-sided, forested valleys, far-reaching views from open hillside near top
SUGGESTED MAP	OS Explorer 152 Newport & Pontypool
START/FINISH	Grid reference: ST228936
DOG FRIENDLINESS	Great dog-walking area, care needed near livestock on Twmbarlwm
PARKING	Cwmcarn Visitor Centre
PUBLIC TOILETS	At visitor centre

It would be difficult to imagine a more transformed landscape than that of the Valleys. Where once slag and spoil heaps towered over bleak villages and greyness appeared to tint everything, there is now every conceivable shade of green, created by mixed forestry clinging determinedly to the steep South Wales hillsides.

The Industrial Revolution had a huge affect on the valleys of South Wales. Limestone, iron ore and coal were found in abundance and in close proximity to each other. Villages and towns sprang up almost overnight and the land that loosely forms the southern boundary of what is now the Bannau Brycheiniog (Brecon Beacons) National Park was changed forever. By the early 20th century, over 250,000 people were employed in South Wales, working more than 600 mines. The Cwmcarn Colliery was originally a downshaft, sunk between 1876 and 1878, for the nearby Prince of Wales Colliery in Abercarn. By 1912, it had become an independent mine, owned by the Ebbw Vale Steel, Iron and Coal Co, Ltd. It was expanded with a second shaft in 1914; an engine wheel, close to the walk, marks the spot. Most of the output was shipped to Newport by canal and from there exported to Europe. The colliery finally closed in 1968.

The landscape, once scarred by years of human toil, have been returned to the community for leisure. The Cwmcarn Forest Drive was opened in 1972, the entrance to which runs over the filled-in mine shafts. Cwmcarn is only one of many parks in the area that have received this treatment. Its crowning glory is the mighty mound of Twmbarlwm, rising to 1,375ft (419m) and enjoying incredible views over the Bristol Channel.

Near Twmbarlwm's characteristic summit – locally known as 'The Tump' or, rather unkindly, 'The Pimple' – are the remains of a hill fort, which is believed to have been constructed by a Celtic tribe called the Silures in the Iron Age or possibly as early as the late Bronze Age. The Silures were a people who lived in the region at the time of the Roman occupation. It is possible that a signalling point was set up here by the Romans, given Twmbarlwm's visibility from great distances away. A motte-and-bailey castle was built at the eastern extreme of the fort, during early Norman times or as late as the 13th century, depending on which authorities you believe. Various legends surround the mountain. One maintains that it is the site of buried treasure that is guarded by bees, while another claims that a giant or great warrior slumbers beneath its soil.

The Cistercian Way is an informal 650-mile (1,046km) circular long-distance footpath, the aim of which is to link all the 17 ancient and modern Cistercian abbeys in Wales. First walked in 1998 by Cistercian enthusiasts, the route uses old roads, trackways and pilgrimage paths as much it can, and where this is not possible, opts for the towpaths of canals and disused Victorian tramways. As it careers along the ridge of Mynydd Maen on its circuitous route from Llantarnam to Risca, the Cistercian Way passes very close to Twmbarlwm.

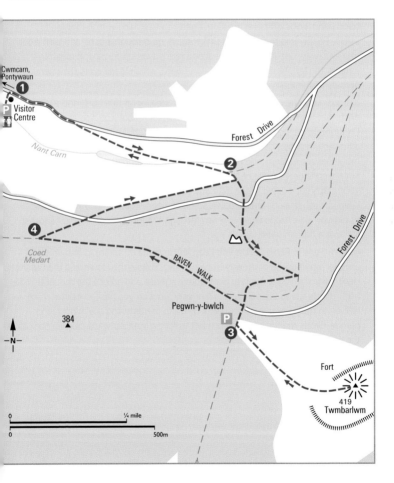

1. From the car park, head up to the visitor centre, and follow the decking around to the right to keep the building on your left-hand side. Go through a gate on to a tarmac footpath and follow this up to Cwmcarn. Walk along either side of the small lake and then, at the far end, continue up a footpath with the stream on your left-hand side. Pass a little pond on a boardwalk and then, at a timber barrier, cross the stream on a tarmac bridge. Bear around to the right and follow the road up the valley, with a steep grassy bank, once a spoil heap, on your left. Above this, you should be able to make out an old winding wheel, which marks the spot of the colliery's second downshaft.

2. Continue over the stream again, then, with a barrier ahead, bear right through a gate to walk uphill on a narrow path. This ends at a gate, which you don't cross; instead, take the second track on the left. This leads on to the tarmac Forest Drive where you turn right and immediately left, to continue uphill on a broad track. As this bends left, bear right to climb up to Forest Drive again. Turn right to follow it down slightly and around a sharp right-hand bend. Fork left here, through a gate, on to a narrow trail that leads uphill. Follow this to the Forest Drive again, go through a gate, and turn right to a four-way junction. Take the second of the two left turns and climb to a gate on the left, next to an information board, which leads on to the open hillside of Twmbarlwm.

3. Go though the gate and follow the track steeply up to a bank and a deep ditch that formed the defensive ramparts of a sizeable Iron Age settlement. Continue to the trig point, from where there are fabulous views to be seen in all directions, then carry on in the same direction to the strange-looking castle mound at the eastern end of the ridge. The purpose of the mound isn't known, but it's considered to be of Norman construction, from around 1070. Retrace your steps back down to the gate and then the four-way junction where you keep almost straight ahead, down some wooden steps, on to a waymarked bridleway. This drops sharply down through the forest to emerge on a forest track at a hairpin bend.

4. Turn right to Forest Drive and keep left to come off the road and on to another waymarked bridleway (Raven Walk). Follow this down and then to the right, near the valley floor, to walk above a fence and across the mountain bike trail. This leads to the stile at the five-way junction you passed earlier. Turn left, on to the narrow path and walk down to the gate and the information plaque. Cross the stream and turn left to follow your outward journey back to the lake and the visitor centre.

Where to eat and drink

There's an excellent café at the visitor centre, which serves up all the usual hot snacks such as soup, jacket potatoes and things with chips, as well as sandwiches and great cakes. For something stronger, try the Castle Lodge in the nearby village of Pontywaun.

What to see

Along with the Cistercian Way, the Raven Walk crosses this route, though it's more formal, and waymarked with a symbol of a raven. It's a 12-mile (19km) circuit taking in the heights around Risca, Cwmcarn, Crosskeys and Ynysddu. Along the route, there are four sculptures of ravens, each one concealing a letter from the ancient Ogham alphabet. If you visit the Green Spaces Caerphilly website, or get hold of the leaflet of the walk, it will help you work out the translation.

While you're there

Caerleon is one of the most significant Roman sites in Europe. It's well worth a visit to see the remains of the centurion's barracks including a well-preserved amphitheatre, of the kind that would have been used to watch gladiators perform, and a complex system of baths that are remarkably well-preserved considering their age. Caerleon is also believed by some to have been King Arthur's court.

WENTWOOD
AND GRAY HILL

DISTANCE/TIME	5.5 miles (8.8km) / 2hrs 30min
ASCENT/GRADIENT	900ft (270m) / ▲ ▲
PATHS	Woodland tracks and bridleways, some sketchy field paths (7 stiles)
LANDSCAPE	Woodland, pastoral valley, bracken-covered hill
SUGGESTED MAP	OS Explorer OL14 Wye Valley & Forest of Dean
START/FINISH	Grid reference: ST428938
DOG FRIENDLINESS	Can run free in woods and on Gray Hill
PARKING	Foresters' Oaks Picnic Site, just north of Wentwood Reservoir
PUBLIC TOILETS	None on route

In the early medieval period, Wentwood forest stretched unbroken from the River Usk to the banks of the Wye, dividing the old kingdom of Gwent into Gwent Is Coed ('Gwent below the wood') and Gwent Uwch Coed ('Gwent above the wood'). East of the Wye, it would have reached as far as the much larger Forest of Dean. At that time, the trees were mainly oak and beech, and provided an ideal habitat for large mammals such as deer and wild boar.

The first sustained assault on Wentwood took place under the Normans, who cleared a large area of forest west of Chepstow to found the settlements of 'Sherriff's Newton' (Shirenewton) and Earlswood. However, the Normans also maintained large areas of the forest as hunting preserves belonging to the lordship of Chepstow. In return for their rent, tenant farmers had the right to collect timber from the forest and let their sheep, goats and pigs to forage for food. Any infraction of these rules was dealt with by a special forest court, which convened twice a year in a grove of oak trees known as 'Foresters' Oaks' (close to the entrance of the picnic site). Criminal offences were dealt with separately, and often severely, and the last recorded hanging at Foresters' Oaks took place in 1829.

Land-hungry farmers and a demand for mature oak trees to build houses and warships led to a further erosion of the woodland area from the 16th century onwards. Ironically, it was the iron industry that saved the heart of the forest, by placing a high value on the timber required for the production of charcoal. However, what remained of the ancient woodland came under intense pressure during World War I, when many native broadleaved trees were felled to provide timber for the trenches. These were largely replaced with conifers, which continue to dominate many areas of the forest. Nevertheless, despite being much reduced in size, Wentwood remains the largest area of ancient woodland in Wales and the ninth largest in the UK.

East of Wentwood, the walk enters a pastoral landscape before climbing steeply west towards the summit of Gray Hill. The hard slog to the top is rewarded by spectacular views across the Severn Estuary and along the

Caldicot Levels, as well as inland over the hills of Wentwood. The hill is well known for its Neolithic and Bronze Age remains, which include standing stones, a stone circle and a D-shaped enclosure. Arthur Machen (1863–1947), author of supernatural, horror and fantasy novels, had a mystical fascination with Gray Hill and featured it in a number of his writings.

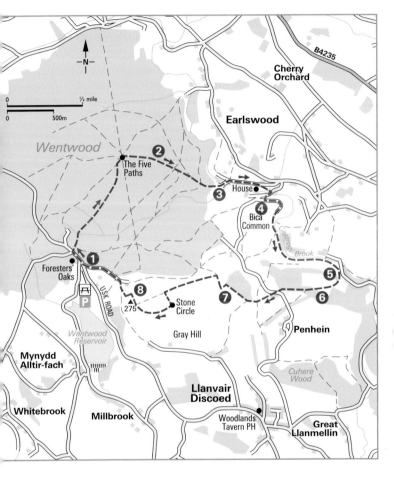

1. Turn left out of the car park and follow the road uphill into Wentwood. Opposite a lane on the left, bear right on to the bridle track signed to Earlswood. Follow the steadily ascending bridleway to a major junction of tracks ('The Five Paths') and turn right. Immediately fork right by a bench.

2. Follow the main forestry track downhill, curving right where a smaller track joins from the left. At a T-junction with another track, keep straight ahead on to a bridleway opposite. Fork left, then left again, to reach a gate out of the woods. Descend on an enclosed path to a ford.

3. Cross a footbridge over the Castrogi Brook on the left, climb to a lane and turn right. Immediately after a house on the right, fork right on to a rough lane. Turn right at a T-junction and descend back towards the Castrogi Brook. Cross the stream and turn immediately left up a footpath signed to Llanfair Discoed.

4. Climb steeply to a lane and turn left. Keep left at a fork and reach a right-hand bend into the garden of a house. Follow waymark arrows down through the garden and bear right alongside the Castrogi Brook. After a short woodland stretch, the path continues along the left-hand boundary of three fields.

5. You will eventually arrive at a gate and stile leading on to a lane. Do not join the lane, but take the footpath climbing to the right ('Gray Hill'). Go through a gap between trees, then bear right to pass a corner of woodland. Maintain direction and climb steeply to a metal gate.

6. Follow a grassy woodland track up to a field and turn right. Join a stony track by a gate and stile and keep ahead to a waymarker post. Turn left and climb to a stile. Continue uphill along the right-hand field edge. Do not cross a gate ahead, but follow the top edge of the field to the left.

7. Cross a stone memorial stile on the right into scrubby woodland. At a clear fork, turn left and climb gently along the ridge until a well-trodden path appears on the left. Descend easily to Gray Hill's prehistoric stone circle, then bear right along a gently climbing path to the summit.

8. Bear slightly right across the summit area on to a waymarked path that descends steeply through bracken. On reaching a bridleway at the base of the common, turn right and continue on to a track and lane. Emerge at a T-junction with Usk Road opposite the entrance to Forester's Oaks Picnic Site.

Where to eat and drink

The Woodlands Tavern in Llanvair Discoed offers a varied menu of freshly prepared and locally sourced food, with a strong emphasis on fish. Light meals and bar snacks are also available, along with a wide range of beers, wines and spirits, and an extensive coffee menu.

What to see

While walking through Wentwood, you will notice a number of areas where conifers have been cleared to allow the native broadleaved forest to regenerate. The Woodland Trust, which acquired a large area of Wentwood in 2006, is working to restore the ancient woodland and improve habitats for wildlife in the forest.

While you're there

Just off the A48 between Newport and Chepstow is the former Roman town of Caerwent. From the western gate car park, you can walk round the town's astonishingly well-preserved walls and wander through the foundations of some of its grandest buildings. These include a Romano-Celtic temple and part of an enormous marketplace and civic hall.

TINTERN ABBEY TO CHEPSTOW

DISTANCE/TIME	8 miles (12.9km) / 3hrs 30min
ASCENT/GRADIENT	820ft (250m) / ▲ ▲ ▲
PATHS	Excellent, waymarked forest tracks and paths
LANDSCAPE	Steep-sided wooded valleys
SUGGESTED MAP	OS Explorer OL14 Wye Valley & Forest of Dean
START	Grid reference: SO533001
FINISH	Grid reference: SO534938
DOG FRIENDLINESS	Care needed on main roads; dogs not allowed in abbey or castle
PARKING	Pay-and-display car park at Tintern Abbey
PUBLIC TOILETS	Car park at start of walk and in car park near Chepstow Castle

The Wye Valley Walk is a 136-mile (218km) waymarked recreational trail that follows the course of the River Wye as it meanders its way between Plynlimon in mid-Wales to Chepstow on the banks of the River Severn. This walk takes in one of the most beautiful sections, full of historic interest, between Tintern Abbey and Chepstow.

Ranking alongside any of Britain's most romantic ruins, Tintern Abbey was only the second Cistercian monastery founded in Britain and the first ever in Wales. Building works began in 1131 and continued on and off right up to its dissolution four centuries later. Its most captivating feature is its Gothic church. This was begun in 1269 and completed 32 years later. The lord of Chepstow Castle, Roger Bigod, rebuilt the church completely in the late 13th century. The monastery flourished, right up until 3 September 1536 when it was surrendered to Henry VIII and unceremoniously dissolved.

Built just a year or two after the Norman Conquest, Chepstow Castle provides an excellent schooling to anyone who wishes to learn about the development of stone castles in Britain. Unusually, the first castle was made of stone, not timber. One of William's most trusted henchmen, William Fitz Osbern, had a keep constructed on a ridge above the river Wye. It is now Britain's oldest surviving stone keep.

Around 1200, a bailey was added by William Marshall in what was then the new-fangled round style, which was less susceptible to damage by whatever missiles might be hurled at it. This innovation was followed up over the following century by the addition of various curtain walls, barbicans and gatehouses, vastly extending the castle until it dominated the entire ridge. Roger Bigod III then added a 'D' tower so strong that the castle was still fit to be used as a defensive position up until 1690 when, after it fell twice to the Roundheads during the War of Three Kingdoms, further adaptations had to be put in place to ward against cannon fire. Today, the castle is at last at peace and is well worth a visit as you come to the end of the walk.

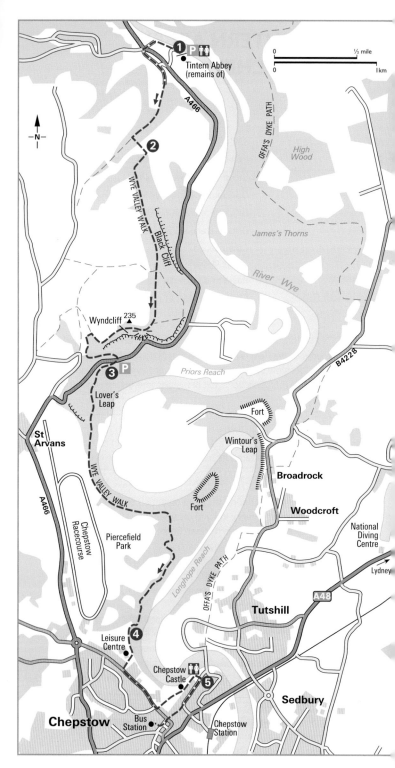

½ mile
1 km

① P 🚻 Tintern Abbey (remains of)

A466

N

High Wood

②

WYE VALLEY WALK

Black Cliff

James's Thorns

River Wye

Wyndcliff 235▲

③ P

Priors Reach

B4228

Lover's Leap

Fort

Wintour's Leap

St Arvans

Broadrock

WYE VALLEY WALK

Fort

Woodcroft

A466

Chepstow Racecourse

Piercefield Park

National Diving Centre

Lydney

Longhope Reach

OFFA'S DYKE PATH

A48

Tutshill

④ Leisure Centre

Chepstow Castle 🚻

⑤

Sedbury

Chepstow Bus Station ●

Chepstow Station

1. The best way to join the Wye Valley Walk (WVW) from the abbey is to head out of the car park and keep straight ahead alongside the river bank on a drive that runs between houses, and then bear left past a converted church. This leads up to the main A466, where you'll see two small lanes heading uphill opposite you. Take the left lane (as you look at them) and follow this uphill until it ends and you bear right up a stony track. Keep heading up through a canopy of beech trees until, after 0.5 miles (800m), you see a waymarker that directs you across a small stream on the left. Cross this and follow the narrow path up to a gate that leads on to an open hillside. Cross the field to another gate that takes you back into the wood.

2. Turn immediately right and the path now steepens and carries you up on to a narrow wooded ridge above Black Cliff. Bear left when it levels to climb steeply again, then continue for another 0.75 miles (1.2km) to a crossroads of paths. Keep straight ahead to continue above Wyndcliff to a fingerpost that directs you to the airy viewpoint of Eagle's Nest. The river curls in a series of meanders and you should be able to see the limestone cliffs of Wintour's Leap on the far bank. These are popular rock climbing crags and also mark the route of the Offa's Dyke footpath, which runs along their tops. Head back up to the main path and continue to a car parking area, where you turn sharp left to go downhill, via a series of zig-zags, to the A466. Cross the road to another car parking area.

3. Keep right, parallel to the road, and locate the path, which at this stage is gravel and runs down into the wood next to a Wye Valley Walk information board. The gravel soon gives way to leaf litter and beechnuts and the noise of the road is quickly left behind as you delve deeper into the wood. After a short and particularly rough section of path, you'll find yourself heading along a narrow terrace above the steep-sided valley. In common with most deciduous woods, there's plenty to capture the imagination at any time of the year, but it's certainly at its best when bathed in the rustic colours of autumn, or in spring when the forest floor is carpeted with flowers and the trees ring with the sound of birdsong. You'll pass behind Piercefield Park and duck into a short, claustrophobic tunnel cut into the rock. Ignore the path off to the right shortly afterwards and continue to a junction with another track, where you turn right then drop to the left of this.

4. A viewpoint by a bench marks the end of the woodland section of the walk and from here, a set of steps leads up to a gap in a wall. Go through and follow the path as it leads behind a leisure centre and out to a car park. Turn left on to the main road and follow it downhill to a narrow park opposite a turning called St Kingsmark Avenue. Turn left on to the waymarked footpath and pass the castle on your left. The Great Tower Keep was built by the Normans in 1067, just one year after the Battle of Hastings. Take time to have a look around and then turn right by the tourist information centre to emerge on Bridge Street.

5. Turn right to climb up through the High Street to the bus station, from where you can catch a bus back to the start. The number 69 bus runs roughly once an hour on weekdays between Chepstow and Tintern.

Where to eat and drink

There are a few establishments in Tintern to choose from but for a drink and decent pub food try the Rose and Crown, or for a cuppa, the Abbey Mill Coffee House is well-placed, close to the abbey ruins. Chepstow has many eateries from cafés and coffee shops to pubs and restaurants for either a quick snack or something more substantial.

What to see

An alternative route for those with a head for heights involves the famous 365 steps that lead down from Wyndcliff. To locate them, follow the path from the Eagle's Nest until you reach a junction by a seat. Turn left here, then right at the bottom to the road. Take this to the Lower Wyndcliff car park and follow the waymarkers.

While you're there

Tintern Abbey was originally founded by Cisterian monks in 1131, although much of it was rebuilt in the 13th century. It operated as a monastic settlement until the 1536 Dissolution, when many of its structures were plundered for building materials. Fortunately, a large number of the graceful arches remain intact and the ruin, in a tranquil riverside setting, is one of Wales's most majestic historic monuments. The romantic scene caught the imagination of the poet William Wordsworth and the artist J M W Turner. It's best to visit at sunrise or sunset and out of the peak holiday seasons.

ABERGAVENNY
AND THE BLORENGE

DISTANCE/TIME	3 miles (4.8km) / 1hr 30min
ASCENT/GRADIENT	530ft (162m) / ▲ ▲
PATHS	Clear tracks over open mountainside, quiet lane
LANDSCAPE	Rugged mountain scenery, huge views over Usk Valley
SUGGESTED MAP	OS Explorer OL13 Brecon Beacons National Park
START/FINISH	Grid reference: SO270109
DOG FRIENDLINESS	Care needed near livestock and on road
PARKING	Small car park at Carn-y-gorfydd
PUBLIC TOILETS	None on route

There's no easier peak to climb in the Bannau Brycheiniog (Brecon Beacons) National Park, but there are also few that occupy such a commanding position. The Blorenge – the English-sounding name probably derives from 'blue ridge' – towers menacingly above the cramped streets of Abergavenny, with the main sweep of the Black Mountains leading away to the north. The mountain actually dominates a small finger of the National Park that points southwards from Abergavenny to Pontypool. It's unique in being the only real peak south of the A465 Heads of the Valleys road. It also marks a watershed between the protected mountain scenery that makes up the bulk of the National Park and the ravaged industrial landscape that forms the southern boundary. Typically, its northern flanks boast a Bronze Age burial cairn and the ground above the escarpment is littered with grass-covered mounds, a remnant of past quarrying. The stone was then transported away on the canals and railways.

Commonly seen as the eastern gateway to the park, even if it sits just outside the boundary, Abergavenny is a thriving market town that owes its success to weaving, tanning and farming. It feels a thousand miles away from the industrial valleys that nudge against its limits from the south. The name, which in Welsh means the confluence of the River Venny, refers to its position at the junction of the River Fenni and the River Usk, but oddly, in Welsh, it's known simply as Y Fenni – the name of the river.

Abergavenny sprang up around a Norman castle that was built to aid efforts by the invaders to rid the area of the Celts. The Welsh proved far more resilient than the Normans had expected and in the end, William de Braose, the lord of the town at the time, resorted to dirty tactics to achieve his aims, such as inviting the Welsh leaders to dinner and then murdering them while they were unarmed. The castle now acts as a museum with some interesting displays of the town's history. Another of Abergavenny's claims to fame is the fact that during World War II, Hitler's deputy, Rudolf Hess, was imprisoned here after his plane crashed in Scotland.

Only 5 miles (8km) south of Abergavenny, but culturally and spiritually a completely different world, Blaenavon tells the full, uncut story of industrial expansion in South Wales. With iron ore, limestone, coal and water all found in local abundance, smelting began here as early as the 1500s, but the town, and the huge iron works that came to dominate it, didn't really get going until the Industrial Revolution of the late 18th century. The colliery, now known as the Big Pit Coal Museum, was founded a full century later than the iron works but closed as a colliery in 1980. It has been immaculately preserved and well organised to give visitors a meaningful insight into the industry itself, the conditions that the people endured and the culture that grew up around them. As well as the engine houses, workshops and the miners' baths, a tour, usually accompanied by an ex-miner as a guide, includes donning a miner's helmet to descend one of the shafts to the actual coalfaces. Blaenavon is considered an exceptional example of industrial South Wales and it was declared a UNESCO World Heritage Site in 2000.

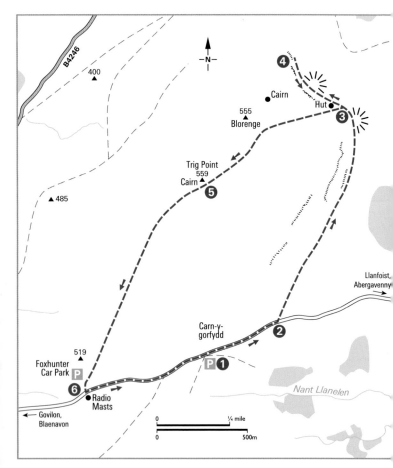

1. From Carn-y-gorfydd Roadside Rest, walk downhill for 500yds (457m) and bear left, through a green barrier, on to a grassy track.

2. This leads easily uphill, through a tangle of bracken, eventually allowing great views over the Usk Valley towards the outlying peak of Ysgyryd Fawr.

3. As the path levels, you'll pass a small locked hut. Continue along the escarpment edge, on one of a series of terraces that contour above the steep escarpment, and enjoy the views over Abergavenny and the Black Mountains. The rough ground was formed by the quarrying of stone.

4. Return to the hut and bear right, on to a faint grassy track that crosses flat ground and a small boggy patch before climbing slightly and becoming stony. Away to the right, you should be able to make out the pronounced hump of a Bronze Age burial cairn. The path now leads easily to the trig point and the huge cairn that marks the summit.

5. Continue in the same direction, drop down past an impressive limestone out-crop and towards the huge masts on the skyline. You should also be able to see the extensive spoil heaps on the flanks of Gilwern Hill, directly ahead. A few hundred yards from the trig point, look out for the tentative beginnings of a grey gravel path (lined, towards the end, with 'Heather and Heritage' waymarkers) that will take you all the way to the car park.

6. At the masts, you'll cross the Foxhunter car park to meet the road where you turn left and continue easily downhill, for 600yds (549m), back to the start.

Where to eat and drink
The Tafarn y Bont in Govilon was built in 1786 and is the main pub in the village. There's also plenty of choice in Abergavenny town and Blaenavon has some good options.

What to see
This is one of the best places in South Wales to see and hear red grouse, which were once managed on these moors. The size of a pheasant, without the long tail, the male is a rusty reddish brown colour and the female more buff and mottled. You'll usually be alerted to their presence by a stabbing, alarmed clucking, followed by a short frantic escape flight.

While you're there
Blaenavon is well worth visiting. As well as the iron works and Big Pit Coal Museum, there's also the incredibly scenic train ride along a short section of the Pontypool and Blaenavon Railway, the highest standard-gauge track in Wales today. It stops off at the Whistle Inn, a nostalgic miner's pub that would have once taken a fair share of the modest wages paid to the men.

47 GOVILON TO LLANFOIST

DISTANCE/TIME	3.5 miles (5.7km) / 1hr 30min
ASCENT/GRADIENT	160ft (49m) / ▲
PATHS	Clear, well-surfaced tracks and paths
LANDSCAPE	Mixed woodland and tranquil canal banks
SUGGESTED MAP	OS Explorer OL13 Brecon Beacons National Park
START/FINISH	Grid reference: SO262134
DOG FRIENDLINESS	Family walkways so scoop the poop
PARKING	Small roadside car park, southwest of Govilon
PUBLIC TOILETS	None on route

This delightful little walk follows the lines drawn by two of the area's main 18th- and 19th-century transport arteries. The outward leg follows the now defunct Merthyr, Tredegar and Abergavenny Railway, often known as the 'Heads of the Valleys Railway'.

In places, the line follows the path of the much earlier Bailey's Tramroad, which ran from Crawshay Bailey's Ironworks at Nantyglo to Govilon Wharf on the banks of the canal. The initial construction, which stretched between Abergavenny and Brynmawr, was started by the Merthyr, Tredegar and Abergavenny Railway Company. This was then acquired by the London and North Western Railway, who were keen to gain a foothold in South Wales. The line opened in 1862 and closed in 1958. It now forms part of the Govilon to Abergavenny Community Route.

The return leg winds along the towpath of the Monmouthshire and Brecon Canal, originally known as the Brecknock and Abergavenny Canal. Built between 1797 and 1812, it represents a remarkable feat of engineering, with over 23 miles (37km) of its total 33 miles (53km) being level, amazing when you think of the mountainous terrain that it traverses. Linking Brecon with Newport and hence the Bristol Channel, the canal was used to transport stone and processed lime from local quarries, including the impressive Llangattock Escarpment, seen from the Black Mountains above Crickhowell.

The canal drifted into disrepair by the 1930s but has been restored by British Waterways, with support from the National Park. It was re-opened for leisure traffic in 1970. However, on 16 October 2007, the canal burst its banks near Gilwern, sending a flood of water down into the Usk valley. People had to be evacuated by from nearby houses. It was declared that a 16-mile (26km) section of the canal would have to be drained in order for the banks to be thoroughly inspected. The repairs took 17 months but the canal was re-opened in early 2009. It is now home to several companies that hire out narrowboats, many of which are electrically powered. These can be charged at various points along the canal and are proving popular with holidaymakers who prefer a form of propulsion slightly less damaging and distinctly quieter than a conventional narrowboat engine.

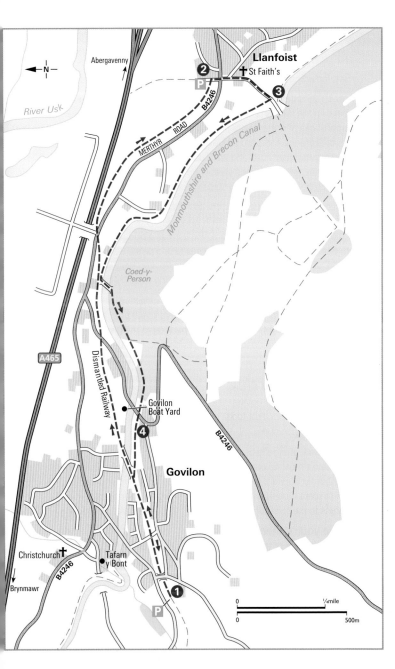

1. A clear tree-covered track runs parallel to the car park. Go through the barrier on to it and turn left. This is now the line of the railway. Follow it beneath a bridge to a residential road and go straight across, around a barrier. Continue behind a row of houses. The path then vaults the canal on a bridge that you should note as it marks the spot where you leave the waterside on the return leg. Continue parallel to the canal for a while, then duck back into

woodland, keeping straight ahead at a junction, waymarked right to the canal. The path passes beneath deciduous trees made up mainly of oak, birch and ash. You're likely to see many small birds, especially those of the garden variety, including most members of the tit family, robins and wrens.

2. About 1.25 miles (2km) after crossing the canal, you'll come to a gate and a car park on the outskirts of the small village of Llanfoist, which grew up on the transport links of the area. Its lime kilns were fed by limestone quarried on the flanks of Blorenge and brought down to the canal by another tramway. Turn right, cross the main road and walk up the lane opposite. This passes the church on the left and climbs steeply up towards the canal. As the lane swings sharply left bear right to climb steps up onto the tow path.

3. Turn right and continue along the bank, which is particularly beautiful in autumn when the magnificent beech woods show off a full spectrum of autumn colours. After about a mile (1.6km), you'll cross a bridge to continue on the south bank, with some canalside houses taking prime waterfront locations opposite. Shortly after this you come to the Govilon Boat Yard, where an interpretation board maps out many interesting facets of the canal's history.

4. Pass the impressive boat yard and another attractive waterside building and then, at the bridge, fork left to follow a well-surfaced path away from the canal and around to the right. This path leads back on to the disused railway where you bear left to follow it back into the residential area and on to the car park.

Where to eat and drink
The Tafarn y Bont in Govilon is a lively, comfortable place, which serves good beer and excellent food, including Sunday roasts.

What to see
As you walk along the banks of the canal, look out for a glimpse of one of Britain's most colourful birds, the kingfisher. In flight, the diminutive little hunter appears less like a bird and more like an ethereal flash of luminescent blue that resembles something from a fairy-tale. It nests in tunnels in the riverbank and generally lays six or seven white eggs.

While you're there
See some more of the canal by either hiring a boat from one of the many operators or alternatively take a half-day cruise from Brecon – Dragonfly Cruises operate from the Canal Basin area near the theatre. It really is a relaxing way to see the countryside.

SUGAR LOAF MKOUNTAIN

DISTANCE/TIME	4.5 miles (7.2km) / 2hrs 30min
ASCENT/GRADIENT	1,150ft (351m) / ▲ ▲ ▲
PATHS	Grassy tracks
LANDSCAPE	Bracken-covered hillsides, secluded valley and rugged mountain top
SUGGESTED MAP	OS Explorer OL13 Brecon Beacons National Park
START/FINISH	Grid reference: SO268167
DOG FRIENDLINESS	Care needed near sheep
PARKING	Northwest of Abergavenny, at the end of lane beyond Sugar Loaf vineyards
PUBLIC TOILETS	None on route

The Sugar Loaf, or Mynydd Pen-y-fal to give it its Welsh name, is without a doubt one of the most popular mountains in the National Park. The distinctive, cone-shaped outline of the rock-strewn summit is visible from miles around and the convenient placing of a car park on the southern flanks of the mountain makes it easy for those who just want to 'climb a mountain'. To follow the well-trodden route is to miss the best of the hill, which, despite its popularity, remains a formidable and dignified peak. This walk takes a more subtle approach, leaving the masses on Mynydd Llanwenarth and dipping into a lonely combe, before making an enjoyable push, up the less-walked west ridge. The steep walls of the valley give a much better sense of scale to the gentle giant you're about to climb. The descent follows the more ordinary route back to the car park.

The Sugar Loaf, and some of the land that surrounds it, belongs to the National Trust, who own around 4 per cent of the land within the National Park. The Trust currently acts as a guardian for over 500 properties and gardens, nearly 620,00 acres (250,00ha) of countryside, including the Bannau Brycheiniog's highest peaks of Pen y Fan and Corn Du, and over 780 miles (1,255km) of coast.

Wales has one of the highest densities of sheep in the world. In the Bannau Brycheiniog (Brecon Beacons) National Park, they outnumber people by 30 to 1. Most of the farms in the National Park are sheep farms. The sheep you'll see while walking across the upland commons are mainly the hardy Welsh mountain sheep, the smallest of the commercially bred sheep with a small head, small ears and a white or tanned face with dark eyes. They thrive in the harsh mountain environment – the ewes spend as many as 36 weeks every year on the high ground – and can eke out food from the very poor grazing available. Typically, the ewes celebrate the New Year by being returned to the hill – around 80 per cent of them will be carrying lambs. They're scanned for twins in February and those carrying two lambs will be retained on the low ground with supplementary food until they've given birth.

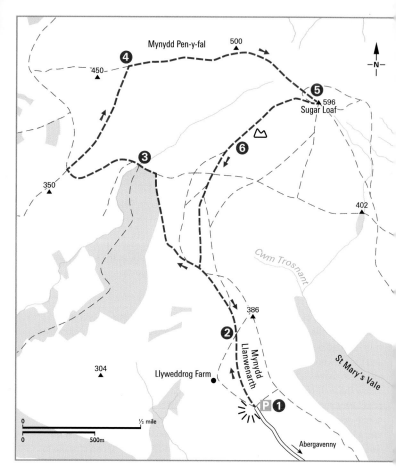

1. Standing in the car park and looking up the slope, you'll see three obvious tracks leading away. The lowest, down to the left, is a tarmac drive; above this, but still heading out left, is a broad grassy track. Take this and follow it for 500yds (457m) to the corner of a dry-stone wall.

2. This marks a crossroads where you keep straight ahead, to follow the wall on your left. Continue along this line for another 0.5 miles (800m), ignoring any right forks, and keeping the wall down to your left. Eventually, you'll start to drop down into a valley, where you leave the wall and head diagonally towards a wood. At the end of the wood, keep left to descend a grassy path to the stream.

3. Climb out of the valley, keeping to the main, steepest, right-hand path. This leads up and around a shoulder and meets another dry-stone wall. Follow this, still climbing a little, until it levels by a corner and gate in the wall. Turn right here, cross some lumpy ground and follow the grassy path up.

4. As the track levels, you'll be joined by another track from the left. Continue ahead and climb on to the rocks at the western end of the summit ridge. Follow the ridge to the white-painted trig point.

5. Looking back towards the car park, you'll see that the hillside is criss-crossed with tracks. Most will lead you back eventually, but the easiest route follows a path that traverses right, from directly below the trig point. This veers left and drops steeply down a blunt spur.

6. Follow this down until it levels and pass two right forks and a path crossing at right angles. As the track veers left, take the right fork to follow an almost sunken track along a broke wall, which leads to a junction by a wall. This is the track that you followed on the outward leg. Bear left and retrace your steps back to the car park.

Where to eat and drink
The best pub in the area is the Dragon's Head at Llangenny, a few miles from the start. Otherwise, Abergavenny has plenty of options including the excellent Trading Post café and the Hen & Chickens pub.

What to see
You'll notice from the signage that the Sugar Loaf, and much of the land that surrounds it, is owned by the National Trust. It's a large area of land but barely a fifth of the Trust's holding in Snowdonia, where it protects over 37,000 acres (14,985ha) of North Wales' dramatic mountain scenery.

While you're there
Between Abergavenny and Monmouth lies a trio of Norman fortifications, White Castle, Skenfrith Castle and Grosmont Castle. They are all open to the public all year except over the Christmas period. White Castle, so named because it was once painted white, is the most impressive and easiest to reach, Skenfrith is in a pretty riverside location and Grosmont sits right on the border with England.

VIEWS FROM YSGYRYD FAWR

DISTANCE/TIME	3.75 miles (6km) / 2hrs
ASCENT/GRADIENT	1,150ft (351m) / ▲ ▲ ▲
PATHS	Tracks through woodland and bracken, steep climb and easy traverse of airy ridge
LANDSCAPE	Mixed woodland, bracken-covered slopes, views over Black Mountains
SUGGESTED MAP	OS Explorer OL13 Brecon Beacons National Park
START/FINISH	Grid reference: SO328164
DOG FRIENDLINESS	Care needed near livestock
PARKING	Small car park on B4521
PUBLIC TOILETS	None on route
NOTES	Do not attempt this walk after a period of prolonged rainfall

Ysgyryd Fawr, or Skirrid Mountain, is the easternmost peak in the Bannau Brycheiniog (Brecon Beacons) National Park. Isolated from the Black Mountains by the Fenni Valley, it's perfectly situated to offer superb views over the rest of the range.

This is a short walk, but it's not to be underestimated; after an easy but enjoyable ramble around the western flanks, the route to the top makes a direct assault on a steep spur that offers little quarter in the fight against gravity. It's definitely worth the effort though, as the summit gives stunning views and the slender ridge that marks the line of descent is one of the finest skyline walkways in the area.

The mountain has long been referred to as the Holy Mountain. The deep cleft in the ridge is said to have been created by a bolt of lightening at the time of the crucifixion and the soil in the valley that divides the hillsides is thought to have special powers. It's even been said to have originated in the Holy Land or, at the very least, Ireland, imported by St Patrick himself. History records local people collecting the soil to sprinkle on anything from coffins to fields of crops. The evangelical importance of the mountain was marked with a small medieval place of worship, dedicated to St Michael, and squeezed on to the narrow summit. Years of mountain-top weather have taken their toll and only the outline plus two small stones that form a doorway remain. There's also evidence of a small hill fort on the same spot. The name Ysgyryd probably derives from Ysgur, Welsh for 'divide', and Fawr meaning 'great' or 'big'. You'll find its little sister Ysgyryd Fach, ('small') a couple of miles further south, on the outskirts of Abergavenny.

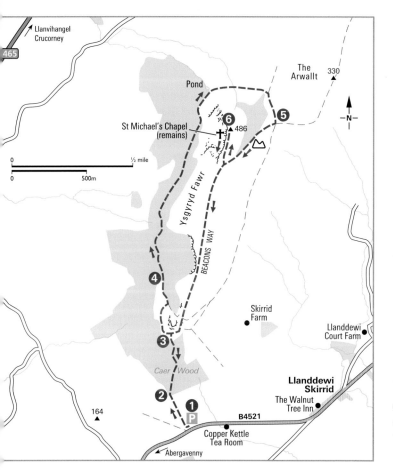

1. Walk through the barrier at the western end of the car park and follow the hedged track around to the right. Climb up to a gate and stile beneath a large oak tree. Cross these and follow the green and white waymarker that directs you off to the right.

2. Ascend a few wooden steps and keep straight ahead at a staggered cross-roads, again following the green and white marker posts. You'll cross a grassy forest track and then climb a series of steps to cross another forest track. Continue to a gate.

3. Turn left here and follow the moss-covered wall around. The wall drops to the left, but continue along the path.

4. This now undulates as it contours around the hillside, eventually leading into a narrow rock-strewn valley. Stay on the main path to pass a small pond on the left and gradually veer around to the right. Stay on the path and you'll emerge on to open ground with a fence to your left. Continue until your way ahead is blocked by a gate.

5. Fork right in front of the gate and follow the open ground steeply uphill. Stay on the main path, following National Trust markers (watch out for the second one, which is very small and off to the right of the path), and eventually you'll reach the top of the ridge. Turn right and follow the ridge for a few paces to the summit.

6. To descend, retrace your steps back to the point where you joined the ridge and then keep straight ahead to the end. Drop down the narrow southern spur and bear around to the right to join a stone path. Follow this down to a wall and bear right to return to the gate at Point 3. Retrace your steps back down through the wood to return to the car park.

Where to eat and drink

Considering how remote it is, there's a couple of good options for this walk. East, in Llanddewi Skirrid, is the Walnut Tree Inn, a smart restaurant with rooms, and to the north, in Llanvihangel Crucorney, there's the Skirrid Inn, purported to be the oldest pub in Wales and also haunted by the ghost of a rebel who was hanged there. For a quick drink and snack, visit the Copper Kettle Tea Room not far from the start of the walk.

What to see

There are a few places on this walk where the path has been constructed using lumps of local stone, laid in such a fashion that vegetation will eventually re-establish itself around them. Footpath erosion is a huge problem across the whole of the Bannau Brycheiniog (Brecon Beacons). Boots destroy vegetation and the thin layer of topsoil is then easily washed away by rainwater, forming deep trenches. It's important to follow these reinforced paths wherever they are found and also to avoid widening any existing tracks by cutting corners or by bypassing puddles and bogs. If you see white bags scattered across the hillsides anywhere, these are full of stone for the paths and have been dropped there by the Ministry of Defence, who use the Beacons for training exercises.

While you're there

Raglan Castle is a few miles east of Abergavenny. Raglan was the last medieval fortification built in Britain and it remains in surprisingly good condition, with an impressive moat and hexagonal Great Tower.

PEN CERRIG-CALCH AND TABLE MOUNTAIN

DISTANCE/TIME	8.5 miles (13.7km) / 4hrs 30min
ASCENT/GRADIENT	1,700ft (518m) / ▲ ▲ ▲
PATHS	Waymarked footpaths, clear tracks, several stiles
LANDSCAPE	Grassy moorland topped with formidable peaks offering great views over deep and remote valleys
SUGGESTED MAP	OS Explorer OL13 Brecon Beacons National Park
START/FINISH	Grid reference: SO234228
DOG FRIENDLINESS	Care needed near livestock, awkward stiles
PARKING	Small lay-by where road crosses Cwm Banw, north of Llabedr
PUBLIC TOILETS	None on route

This walk climbs on to Table Mountain, which is topped with the remains of a most spectacularly positioned fortress. It then scales the steep escarpment above to cross Pen Cerrig-calch. Following a superb lofty traverse of another formidable peak, Pen Allt-mawr, the walk descends a broad ridge that forms the western wall of the remote Grwyne Fechan valley.

Towering above the mountain hub of Crickhowell, Table Mountain appears as a flat-topped knoll tucked beneath the white screes of Pen Cerrig-calch. It is topped by the ramparts of an impressive Iron Age fort known as Crug Hywel, which translates to 'Hywel's Fort.' Hywel was a significant figure in Welsh history in the 10th century. The grandson of Rhodri the Great, who killed the leader of the Viking invaders at Anglesey, he made huge strides towards the unification of the infant nation and also gained much acclaim for the introduction of a system of rules, which became known as the Law of Wales. The rules, aimed at freeing the common man from the scruples of rich and powerful merchants, gave improved rights to women as well as placing values on everyday items such as domestic cats. He became known as Hywel Dda, or Hywel the Good. Although Hywel reigned in the 10th century, the fortifications on the hilltop are probably 1,000 years older. He may have taken advantage of the naturally defended position at some stage.

Standing guard over Crug Hywel is the 2,300ft (701m) peak of Pen Cerrig-calch. It is unique as the highest limestone peak in a landscape that comprises mainly old red sandstone. The name says it all; cerrig is stone and calch is lime. Although it appears now to be an isolated pocket of the soft white rock, it would have once been linked to the larger tract south of the Usk.

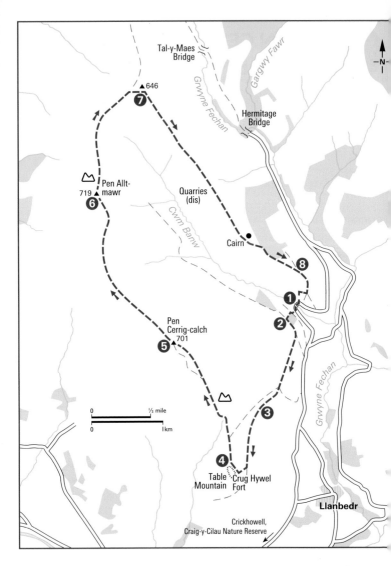

1. Walk back over the bridge and bear right up the ramp that leads to the second gate on the right. Cross the stile up some steps to the right of the gate and walk up the edge of a field to another stile that leads on to a lane. Cross this and climb over another stile to continue, with a wood on your left, up to yet another stile in a dry-stone wall.

2. Cross this and turn left to follow a faint path around the hillside through the bracken. Walk alongside the wall to a clear off-set crossroads, where the wall drops away, keep straight ahead here and at the next crossroads rejoin the wall shortly. Continue straight across another section where the wall drops away and then joins the path again.

3. Next time it drops, keep straight ahead again to meet it at a pronounced corner of a field with two buildings at its foot. Turn right on to a clear track that leads straight up on to the summit of Table Mountain.

4. Turn off the plateau at its narrowest northern point and cross the saddle on an obvious track. This climbs steeply up on to Pen Cerrig-calch. As the path levels, ignore a track to the left and keep straight ahead until you reach the trig point.

5. Continue ahead to drop slightly down a small crag to meet the escarpment edge. Continue along the ridge, which narrows slightly, then climb again to the narrow summit of Pen Allt-mawr.

6. A path leads down the steep northern spur. Take this and cross flat, open and often wet ground towards a small hump ahead. As you start to climb, you'll come to a parting of the paths.

7. Fork right here and continue to a small cairn on the top of a narrow ridge that leads southeast. Follow the ridge easily down until you eventually cross some quarried ground and come to a large cairn. Keep straight ahead to walk down to a stile marked 'Footpath Only No Bikes' at the top of a plantation. Cross this and keep straight ahead again to follow the rutted track alongside two sides of the plantation. Where the third side drops away to the left carry straight on over a field, eventually meeting a wall to your right that takes you down to a track between walls where you pass through a gate.

8. Go downhill to a junction of paths. Keep straight ahead, through a gate, and head along the top of the field to a marker post that sends you left, downhill. Bear left at the bottom to a stile by a gate. This leads back to the lay-by.

Where to eat and drink

The Bear Hotel in Crickhowell is the choice of the eating and drinking establishments in town, but there are other options too.

What to see

The tiny town of Crickhowell makes a splendid base for exploration. There are remains of an impressive Norman fortification in the town itself. This was built in the 11th century and became famous after it was attacked by Owain Glyndwr in his uprising of the 1400s. The town's most beautiful feature is the 16th-century bridge over the River Usk.

While you're there

Craig-y-Cilau Nature Reserve lies just south of Crickhowell. It features a long limestone crag at 400ft (122m) and there's also a raised bog, woodland and a complex cave system.

Explore
the UK at
RatedTrips.com

AA